CONTEMPORARY
POETRY OF
NEW ENGLAND

EDITED BY

ROBERT PACK

JAY PARINI

CONTEMPORARY POETRY OF NEW ENGLAND

MIDDLEBURY COLLEGE PRESS

Published by University Press of New England

Hanover and London

Middlebury College Press

Published by University Press of New England, Hanover, NH 03755

Printed in the United States of America

5 4 3 2 1

Library of Congress Cataloging-in-Publication Data

Contemporary poetry of New England / edited by Robert Pack, Jay Parini.
    p. cm.
  ISBN 0–87451–965–9 (cloth: alk. paper) ISBN 0–87451–966–7 (pbk.
alk. paper)
   1. American poetry—New England. 2. American poetry—20th century.
3. New England—Poetry. I. Pack, Robert, 1929– II. Parini, Jay.
PS541 .C66 2002
811'.5080974—dc21   2001008179

Grateful acknowledgment is made for permission to reprint the following poems:

Julia Alvarez, "Addison's Vision," copyright © 2001 by Julia Alvarez. Reprinted by permission of Susan Bergholz Literary Services, New York. All rights reserved.

Peter Balakian, "Robert Lowell Near Stockbridge," "A Country House," and "Parts of Peonies," originally published in *June-Tree: New and Selected Poems, 1974–2000*, Harper Collins.

Philip Booth, "Beyond Equinox," "Within," and "Coming To," originally published in *Lifelines: Selected Poems, 1950–1999*. Viking.

T. Alan Broughton, "A Season's Edge," in *Tar River Poetry*; "Ice Fisher," in *The Literary Review*; "First Snow, Deep Sleep, As Always," in *Virginia Quarterly Review*; and "Cidertime," in *Abraxas 5 Anthology*.

Rosellen Brown, selected poems, originally published in *Cora Fry's Pillow Book*, Farrar, Straus & Giroux, 1994.

David Budbill, "Another Kind of Travel," "North is Nowhere," and "Quiet and Seldom Seen," from *Moment to Moment: Poems of a Mountain Recluse*. Copyright © 1999 by David Budbill. Reprinted with the permission of Copper Canyon Press, P. O. Box 271, Port Townsend, WA 98368–0271.

John Canaday, "Spring Cleaning," in *Bostonia Magazine*; "New England Ghazal," in *Harvard Review*.

Peter Davison, "Falling Water," "Farmer and Wife," and "Like No Other," originally published in *Breathing Room*, Knopf, 2000. "Homage to Robert Frost" reprinted with the permission of the author.

Acknowledgments continued on page 221

Contents

Introduction   xiii

Julia Alvarez   Addison's Vision   1

Peter Balakian   Robert Lowell Near Stockbridge   2
                         A Country House   3
                         Parts of Peonies   4

Jennifer Bates   Our Town: Middlebury, Vermont   5
                         Storm   7

Philip Booth   Beyond Equinox   9
                         Within   10
                         Coming To   10

T. Alan Broughton   A Season's Edge   12
                         Ice Fisher   12
                         First Snow, Deep Sleep, As Always   15
                         Cidertime   15

Rosellen Brown   From *Cora Fry's Pillow Book*   17

David Budbill   Another Kind of Travel   22
                         North Is Nowhere   22
                         Quiet and Seldom Seen   23

John Canaday   Spring Cleaning   24
                         Stock   25
                         New England Ghazal   26

Lesley Dauer   Nocturne   28
                         The Playground   28
                         Lonesome Is a Curious Word   30

Peter Davison	Falling Water	32
	Farmer and Wife	33
	Homage to Robert Frost	34
	Like No Other	35
Greg Delanty	A Wake on Lake Champlain	36
	Vermont Aisling	36
	The Great Ship	37
Mark Doty	American Sublime	38
	Time on Main	39
John Engels	Bleeding Heart	41
	Raking the Leaves	42
	Perennials	43
	Moving from Williston	44
	Storm	46
Carol Frost	Country	47
	Flicker	48
	Winter Poem	49
	Eel Spearing	50
Richard Frost	The Change	51
	The Hill	51
Jeffrey Harrison	Horseshoe Contest	53
	Not Written on Birch Bark	55
Laban Carrick Hill	False Consciousness	56
	Duck Blind	56
David Huddle	Idaho Once	58
	Got Power?	59
	The Nature of Yearning	60
Cynthia Huntington	Hot Wind, Provincetown Harbor	63
	Sea-Meadow	64

Richard Jackson	The Angels of 1912 and 1972	66
	Villanelle of the Crows	67
	No Fault Love	68
Erica Jong	Keep Back the Dark	70
Richard Kenney	Starling	71
	Driving Sleeping People	72
	Plume	73
	Apples on Champlain	74
Galway Kinnell	Trees	76
Maxine Kumin	The Exchange	79
	The Potato Sermon	80
	Skinnydipping with William Wordsworth	81
Sydney Lea	Inviting the Moose: A Vision	83
	Yoked Together	84
	Well, Everything	86
Brad Leithauser	North-Looking Room	88
Gary Margolis	Slow Words for Shoreham and the Apple Blossom Derby	89
	First Spring	90
	Elegy in Case They Win	91
	Rough Flight into Boston	91
	While We Are Waiting	92
Paul Mariani	North/South	94
	Mountain View with Figures	95
	Landscape with Dog	95
	New England Winter	96
	A Break in the Weather	97
Cleopatra Mathis	Gatekeeper	99
	The Owl	99
	Intermediary	100

Gardner McFall	Seaweed Weather	102
	Album	102
	In Mountain Air	103
Wesley McNair	Driving North in Winter	104
	The Unspoken	105
	What They Are	105
	Shovels	106
Nora Mitchell	Starling	108
	Flowering Tree	108
	Lilies	109
	Listening through Snow	110
Susan Mitchell	The Grove at Nemi	112
	Pussy Willow (An Apology)	113
	The Kiss	115
Nancy Nahra	Being Without Power	118
	In a Northern Spring	119
	Conundrum, Maine	119
	Rocky Shore	120
Alfred Nicol	On the Strand at Plum Island	121
	Wide Brush	122
	Salt Marsh	122
	March Winds	123
Carole Simmons Oles	Old Couple at Howard Johnson's Soda Fountain in Manchester, New Hampshire	124
	At Boston Public Library	125
	On the Cliff Walk at Newport, Rhode Island, Thinking of Percy Bysshe Shelley	126
	Apple-Picking	126
	After Fire in Ripton, Vermont	127
April Ossmann	Living Without	129
	Red Glove	130
	January Thaw	132

Robert Pack	Baled Hay	133
	Wild Turkeys in Paradise	133
	Late Summer Purple	135
	Mountain Ash Without Cedar Waxwings	135
	Ode to a Lovesick Moose	137
Jay Parini	Swimming in Late September	139
	Skater in Blue	139
	The Lake House in Autumn	140
	A Killing Frost	140
	The Ruined House	141
Joel B. Peckham, Jr.	When I Dream of Eternity	145
	Mud Season	145
	Cage Cry—Sharon, Massachusetts	146
Kevin Pilkington	Woodstock, Vermont	148
	A Spruce in Vermont	149
Verandah Porche	Villanelle in April	151
	September at the Home	151
Lawrence Raab	The Garden in Winter	153
	Emily Dickinson's House	153
	Hunters	154
Ira Sadoff	The Horse Wanted Sugar	156
	I Join the Sparrows	156
	I Like Waking Up	157
Mary Jo Salter	Spring Thaw in South Hadley	158
	Reading Room	159
	The Upper Story	161
Neil Shepard	Autumn Progress: Rural Vermont	165
	Trusting the Land's Pure Curve	166
	From Hayden's Shack, I Can See to the End of Vermont	168

Jane Shore	"Public Service Is Rich Enough"	172
	Fairbanks Museum and Planetarium	173
Robert Siegel	Spring Peepers	177
	Looking for Mt. Monadnock	178
	Walden Once More	179
Diane Swan	Afterbirth	181
	Elmwood Cemetery	181
	Cold	183
	Wild Cedars	184
John Tagliabue	From the *Maine Notebooks*	185
	Two Poems	187
	Three Notes Related to the January Snow Storm	188
Sue Ellen Thompson	Connecticut in March	191
	Compass	192
Pauls Toutonghi	9 P.M. Storm	193
	Morning	193
	Lightning Scars the Sugar Maple	194
Ellen Bryant Voigt	A Brief Domestic History	195
	The Art of Distance, I	196
	Ravenous	197
	Dooryard Flower	198
Rosanna Warren	Island in the Charles	200
	Day Lilies	201
	March Snow	202
Emily Wheeler	Low Blue Fire	203
	Visiting My Parents: Natick, Massachusetts	203
	Snow in New Hampshire	204

Richard Wilbur	Zea	205
	Mayflies	206
	Signatures	206
	Crow's Nests	207
Nancy Willard	The Exodus of Peaches	209
Baron Wormser	The Pump	211
	Cheerful	212
	Time of Year	213
	Building a House in the Woods, Maine, 1971	214

List of Contributors   217

Introduction

Robert Pack and Jay Parini

The English writer G. K. Chesterton once meditated on the place of "place" in a writer's mind: "There is at the back of every artist's mind something like a pattern or type of architecture. The original quality in any man of imagination is imagery. It is a thing like the landscape of his dreams; the sort of world he would like to make or in which he would wish to wander; the strange flora and fauna of his own secret planet, the sort of thing he likes to think about. This general atmosphere, and pattern or structure of growth, governs all his creations, however varied." Not surprisingly, this landscape at the back of a writer's mind often refers to somewhere he or she happens to live, or once lived—a geographical place that made a deep impression on the writer's imagination.

In his notebooks, Robert Frost once remarked to himself, as if as admonition or exhortation: "Locality gives art." With the ferocity of a great artist, he was able to limit himself and his material in radical ways that opened up those limits, allowing him (and, by consequence, the reader) to push beyond those limits. Like William Faulkner and John Steinbeck, two of his great contemporaries, Frost understood that a writer often (not always) achieves universality in literature by concentrating his or her focus, by circumscribing a small world, whether it be a rural Mississippi county, a neglected but gorgeous valley in central California, or that area Frost referred to as "north of Boston."

The region commonly known as New England—one of the oldest settlements on this continent—has influenced American writers from the time of its Puritan beginning, supplying a vast array of deep and moving images. This region has a rich and complex history going back to its indigenous population, which was largely (and sometimes violently) displaced by European invaders. In the nineteenth century, New England became a primary region for intellectual work of a very high order. The center of the Transcendental movement was, of course, located in Concord, Massachusetts, and New England as a whole became a major locale for what has been called the American Renaissance—a period of unusual productivity for poets, novelists, and essayists. One associates a large cluster of first-rate writers with this period: Longfellow, Dickinson, Hawthorne, Emerson, Thoreau, and Melville each had close connections to this part of North America, and each contributed to our imaginative possession of this region.

In the twentieth century, beginning with Frost and Edwin Arlington Robinson, the states of Massachusetts, Connecticut, Rhode Island, New Hampshire, Vermont, and Maine have contributed a dazzling array of writers. The region has virtually teemed with poets, native-born and (rather commonly) imported. What these poets have done is make the landscape and history of this region their own; their poems have grown from, and contributed to, the landscape and history before them in a complicated process, as the connections between language and reality have been explored—a process most beautifully articulated by one of New England's greatest poets, Wallace Stevens, who put the "war between the mind and sky" at the center of his own project in poetry.

New England is a region of vast differences, of course, ranging from extremely rural parts to industrial areas. Not surprisingly, one often associates certain poets with particular areas. Robert Lowell, for example, wrote often about Boston and the North Shore, where his family came from. James Merrill lived for many years in Stonington, Connecticut, a seaport town, and his poems often reflected the imagery and atmosphere of Water Street. Wallace Stevens wrote "An Ordinary Evening in New Haven," putting that town on the heavily populated map of literary New England. Richard Eberhart—a native of Minnesota—spent much of his life in New Hampshire and Maine, and his work deeply reflected these localities. Even that great Southerner, Robert Penn Warren, spent a good deal of his life in Vermont, where he owned a home in West Wardsboro, and his late wonderful burst of creative activity owed much to his residence there. The poems of his last thirty years were rooted in this state, and in the landscape of Connecticut, where he also had a house. Examples multiply at every turn of the eye.

This collection of recent poems about New England is a testament to the enduring power of the region as a source of inspiration for poets. It was Shakespeare, in *A Midsummer Night's Dream,* who famously declared that the purpose of poetry was to give to "airy nothing / A local habitation and a name." An astonishing variety of poets found this piece of America worthy of imaginative possession. Many were born and raised here, but others—Julia Alvarez, for example, who was born in the Dominican Republic—have come from far away to find the ambience of rural New England uniquely hospitable, a place where creativity was encouraged, where the landscape itself was conducive to meditation of the kind essential for the making of poems.

Readers will find a wide array of poets in this volume. Many are well known, and long associated with the region, such as Richard Wilbur, Philip Booth, David Budbill, Peter Davison, Galway Kinnell, Mark Doty, Mary Jo Salter, Brad Leithauser, Baron Wormser, and Maxine Kumin; others are less well established. Indeed, this volume teems with younger writers, such as Jennifer Bates, Jeffrey Harrison, Pauls Toutonghi, Emily Wheeler, Alfred Nichol, and Nora Mitchell. These writers have only begun to find an audience for their work, and this volume will help in establishing them as voices with considerable resonance.

What we, as editors, found surprising in the work of assembling this collection was the variety of styles and forms that have been employed. While each of these poems draws sustenance, Antaeus-like, from a particular piece of ground, the similarity stops there. Each poet, in his or her own measure and pace, reflects on, transmogrifies, the elements of regionality. These elements, however, give a striking unity to the volume, as each poet offers a further brush stroke, helping to define a region that has within its strictures a remarkable variety of landscapes and weathers, cultural traditions, and linguistic habits.

Contemporary Poetry of New England offers a vivid portrait of a region, its colors and smells, its physical and emotional textures, and the people who make a life in its isolated valleys and remote hills, its small towns, its busy urban centers. It presents a range of poets, few of whom would call themselves a "regional poet," although each has taken to heart in a private way Frost's haunting dictum: "Locality gives art." It does, and the results will be found in these pages.

CONTEMPORARY
POETRY OF
NEW ENGLAND

ADDISON'S VISION

Addison tells of spending his summer
clearing the farm his family has owned
since the revolutionary war
acres and acres of overgrown fields—
pastures and hayfields, hedgerows, forest growth—
a big enterprise for an ex-farm boy
turned minister in a flowing cassock
not handy for plowing. I've seen him lift
the bread and wine in pale hands above
the bowing heads of his parishioners.

And as he tells about his summer work
I see the chalice turn into a saw,
the handle darkened with his father's sweat,
and before that, his grandfather's, on down
the generations until the sad phrase
delivered in the garden comes to mind:
"sweat of your brow," which now is Addison's,
clearing the land so that we see the light
as it first shone on Adam, pruning turned
into a kind of hands-on ministry.

What did he see once the hedgerows were cleared?
The skies opening, divine light beaming down
on distant vistas of a promised land?
Salvation for God's sweating minister?
But he saw only what was there to see—
rolling green hills such as a child might draw,
cars moving on a distant road like beads
on an abacus, a neighbor hanging wash:
the earth released and grown so luminous
that he was saved simply by seeing it.

ROBERT LOWELL NEAR STOCKBRIDGE

The traffic thinned past Chicopee.
Farmland hardened and recalled
Edwards and his relic oak

where a spider set its web
in your heart before you left the Alps.

In the red light of maples
where Taylor once sang
at a wasp pinned in a net

you left your insects for the test
in rotten hollow logs,

and the knot God made in Paradise
tightened on the hills.

Your eye flushed out
on a September morning,
when trees were stitched with webs
too fine to see,

and spiders swam the air
and turned to glisten.

Invisible filaments your heart
gave way before—
a Berkshire hawk dove on them

and left the maples
in their beauty
untenable as gristle.

A COUNTRY HOUSE

Late November and I am
in a country house.
The moon glares across
an open field and there's

a lump of deer guts
like a shapeless sculpture.
The air keeps cutting
at the stubble I can't see.

I've been in the eaves
and found I couldn't stay.
The beams are simple timbers
made of simple trees.

The wind in the eaves
breaks some shingles loose,
and I want a deer to rise
from the pile of himself.

I'm a man in a country house.
Flanks and splints of oak are all
that keep the night off my back.
Outside the ground turns

harder than a skull,
and some deer walk
into the eye-holes of the night.
A son must face a treeless place,

a country house held up
by trunks and branches older than man.

Things out there are still.
My father's doesn't walk on the earth.

PARTS OF PEONIES

It rained so much in June
some grew to look like stuffed cabbage
or the small heads of lambs.

Even the stigmas were buried
in the dense red and white.

All day I tried to put
my hands into their swollen insides.
I thought my touch would reawaken.

In the slightest breeze
they swooned
and things fell out—

(their nectar glands
sweet and white on my hands)

the spongy sac of a goat,
the shard of a wooden belfry,
quills and the bark of a eucalyptus,

and here in my small upstate garden,
a bladder and a nest are the same,

a bird drops eggs everywhere.

I close my eyes in the harsh light,
and the black spots become peonies.

OUR TOWN: MIDDLEBURY, VERMONT

I.

Flight is the best way back I know.
Leave in the evening, as the sky,
balanced between darkness and light,
shrinks to fit the porthole window
you lean your face against,

watching the city that lies below
like a heap of jewelry, stripped
from throat and ears and dropped
onto a dress someone slid from her hips,
black silk beneath the diamonds' glow.

The plane touches down in Burlington.
If you've chosen to travel in winter,
the snow will glitter, a sheet of white
as clean as the narrow sheets someone
placed on the bed you will sleep in tonight.

2.

There must have been clear and quiet days
I spent at the public library in town,
but in my mind, I only hear wind
and rain, fierce outside the windows,
drowning the sounds of the street.

Inside, I sit in a leather chair
with a book pressed open in my lap.
As I bend over the page, my hair
shadows that smooth snow fractured
by animal tracks, a dotted map

I am diligently learning to read.
When I lick a finger and turn a page,
the crisp edge catches against my skin,
drawing blood. I lick the salty smear.
The book shuts between my knees.

3.

Mrs. Swift was the oldest woman in town.
Every Sunday she sat in her pew at church,
her tiny monkey's skull swathed in down
and topped with a frail black hat.
She moved like an arthritic cat,

watching each time her small foot landed
as she traveled down the aisle.
I watched our youthful priest
approach respectfully, the Eucharist
cradled like water in his careful hands.

At the town's bicentennial celebration
on the village green, he told me
that Mrs. Swift had been just my age
when the hundredth birthday of our nation
was celebrated in Middlebury.

4.

According to playground legend,
a passage runs underneath Main Street
from building to building, including
those linked above by the bridge
over Otter Creek. The fugitives

hid underneath the crashing falls
as they paused for breath in their flight
to Canada and freedom. Walter
was always claiming he had crawled
through the narrow darkness into light

somewhere on the other side.
Sometimes we agreed to take
his story for the truth,
pretending for his sake and ours
we didn't know he'd lied.

5.

In Middlebury's production of *Our Town,*
three local churches served as the stage:
Baptist for the first act; Methodist, the second;
and St. Stephen's Episcopal (mine) for the third.
Between the acts, we followed ushers

who carried lanterns past stages vignettes:
two lovers spooned behind the bandstand on the green,
a horse and buggy meandered down the street,
and in the window of the barber shop
a barber stood with razor and strop

and a customer stretched out and lathered up—
my friend Peter, a native Vermonter
among all these actors from New York.
When the invisible curtain fell at the end
(for a church isn't really a stage, any more
than Peter was a customer in that well-lit room)

we twisted in our seats and sighed.
And went home.

STORM

after Approaching Storm: Beach near Newport *by Martin Johnson Heade*

I have never lived by the sea.
I have never walked along the water's edge,
footprints briefly engraved on the sand,
small waves nipping my ankles
like the cat when he wants his dinner.
The salt air comes through my window

over city streets, inland.
There is concrete under my feet.
But the storm—black sky crowding
yellow down to the horizon—
the storm I recognize.
In a parking lot in Boston,
a flock of birds passed over me,
blurred thumbprint on the massing clouds.
The hair on the back of my neck
moved with wind, blood
surged in my heart's closed chambers
and held out my arms
as I hold them open now to you.
I'm your natural disaster, your
rush of water and salt,
your last light on the rocks
as the sun disappears
and the electric air moves in.

BEYOND EQUINOX

Still weeks to ice-out
in upcountry lakes. Here
on the coast, salt-ice

gets lifted off coves
by gales and steep wave-
lengths. Tides flow hard

between the mainland
and islands. Out in
the Thorofare, two fish-

boats, blurred in thin rain,
march back and forth like
small boys' small toys.

Off Stump Cove, a red boat
and yellow boat slowly
wallow, dragging the bottom

for scallops. Across
old tides, Deer Isle and
Little Deer loom tall as

spruce, dark as deer in
their winter coats. At
the end of whatever

day this is, a sky
like pleated gray silk
begins to glint with

thin gold caught behind it:
this last day of March
or April Fools' first.

WITHIN

A peninsula church, October's last Sunday.
Outside, a half-gale. Barely beyond the twelve-
over-twelve high panes of the Southwest window,

frost-paled maple leaves, still stemmed to
their half-stripped tree, stream a bright translucence.
Sunstruck, cloudstruck, horizon-bound by

the seawind, they outshone the sermon, the hymns,
the words of the congregation's oldest prayer.
Given the leaves' light, their benediction, matched

by the Bach *partita* fallen or risen to us through
its thousand seasons, we feel our lives bare: without
guilt or reason, we let our eyes fill and be lifted.

COMING TO

Coming to woods in light spring rain,
I know I am not too late.
     In my week
of walking down from White Mountains,
I dreamt I might die before
familiar woods woke me.
     Come slowly,
the way leaves come, I've arrived at
their turnings: from bronze, gold, wine,
to all greens, as they let sun in
to tug them toward light.

                    Come again now
to woods as they've grown, hardwood
and soft, birch, hemlock, and oak,
I walk into my boyhood,
                         back to
my mother,
                the mother who took me in hand
to steer me across back fields to the woods.
Over and over, she slowed to give me
the local names: swampmaple, shadblow,
hackmatack, pine.
                      Given those woods,
trees renewed in me now, I've begun
to know I'm older than all
but the tallest stands.
                          Under trees,
I discover my mother's old namings
beginning to bloom: bloodroot,
hepatica, bunchberry, trillium;
                            in air
so quiet the flowers barely move,
I shiver a little, over and over.
I listen to troutlily, violet, jack-
in-the-pulpit, spring beauty.

I let my head bow as I name them.

A SEASON'S EDGE

Pruning the apple tree I scatter
its suckers and twigs across wet snow.
March wind honeycombs the drifts,
and when my work is done I stand
in an attic window close
to spume of driven clouds.

I have climbed steep stairs in an ancient city,
caressing her hair and breasts
even before we lay in a low-eaved room.
The earth we rose away from clung
as if we had roots like grass and bush below.

High on a limb I gripped the crowning branch
but did not cut its last reach for sky.
My hands, tangled in her strands,
curved to the shape of her head above me.

Wind shook the panes and we climbed
till our cries touched invisible fruit,
higher than we could reach.

ICE FISHER

I pay out line until it slackens
I'm not into catching anymore.
Used to tote a full pail
when I trudged home over the snow,
but I got sick of the taste
of perch, would give them away,
then quit. Besides, I don't know
the neighbors now. Never was

the tug and hauling in
and scraping scales that took me.
I like pounding together a shack,
hauling it out, then squatting
over the hole I bore,
alone with a patch of clear ice
and sometimes wind that scratches up
drifts on the walls. So now
I don't have to pay for bait.
Sometimes I wonder what fish think
of empty hooks, lead on a string
sinking to the coldest rock.
But they don't think. Nothing
behind those agate eyes.

One winter a truck fell through.
I was too far away,
heard the spin and whine,
went out to look, saw the ice
still giving, cab going last
where a window was half down,
a figure howling, gone.
I ran but couldn't get too close.
No one came up. I marked
the spot where already a skin
of ice was forming. Next day
it was zero again. Diver
went down, said the two men's
faces were at the window
waiting. Spring, when they hauled
the truck on a barge, they found
the door had stuck. But the worst
was later that winter day
when they sent the diver down
again to try for the bodies.
Trouble announced itself
in his slack rope. They tugged,
left it dangling, kept the hole
open, punched out others
in a widening circle. All night

they axed the ice, shone spotlights.
Only so much air in tanks.
By morning they gave it up.

Thing is, when you lose the rope
in the dark far under ice
and you panic for only a moment,
or say the cold has numbed
your brain before the shock
wakes you when you touch
your waist and miss the tether
and look around to see no truck,
just dull water and far above a grayish light,
you are lost in a world
with heavy lid between you and sky.
When your head beats against ice
you've met the limit. Your fists pound
until you remember to stay calm,
save the stuff on your back.
Swim slowly along, upside down,
hands groping. Here a brighter glow
seems hopeful, or a crack, but ice
can heave and flaw and mend
again to leave a scar, a window
you can't break. The light dims.
Finally everywhere is black.
You are free to move anywhere
but up. You can even scream.

They never found him. I dreamed
once that I cleared the ice
in my hut and he was staring up.
Between us the solid glass
had no flaws, not even trapped bubbles.
His mouth formed slow words,
I put my ear against the cold.
The side of my head grew numb.
Tell me, tell me, I tried to say
but nothing left my throat. When I looked
again I was looking up to myself

looking down and I flattened my hands
as he did. Palm to palm we turned
slowly with ice between us.
I could tell no difference.

In summer I pay no mind
to the lake. Let them sail or whip
their skis into spray. I see
the waves. I see the sun fall down.
I'll even walk to the pier to watch.
Who talks to an old man feeding gulls?
All I'm saying is that winter
in my shack with an empty line,
no one to trouble me,
the lake as still as it can be,
I'm almost there.

FIRST SNOW, DEEP SLEEP, AS ALWAYS

He lights a fire, cups coffee
in his hands and sits by the window.
The cats perch on the sill
to watch birds at the feeder,
a squirrel below. The empty rooms
sometimes shudder with rising steam,
hisses the house makes against the cold.
He thinks this room, his figure in its chair,
the watchful cats, have been gently turned
by a giant hand, and down the glass ball
that surrounds them, white things
fall and fall.

CIDERTIME

The apples rot,
the last sun

mocks
with gaudy leaves,
and even wind
is only paddling
in the air.
This is the easy time
for bees
whose labor
through the summer
kept them hefting
juice
in ceaseless portage.
Now the comb
is full,
frost blunts
all urgency of search
and nothing is left
to serve
except the self.
Waylaid by apples,
they batten to the juice,
sway on the edge
of pulpy clefts
and drink and drink
until their pale wings
droop.
There is no duty,
no need for return.
They've earned
these apples
soft and fallen
that earth offers,
then reclaims.

FROM CORA FRY'S PILLOW BOOK

They need a sign: **No mothers in the body shop!**
I call out "Chip!" and my voice is a dropped wrench, loud
as I can make it. In the dead light, motes swirling, standing still,
caught in its oil, black rags, sour iron smell, the hissing and clanging,
through it all I can barely make out his features. And he turns away in
    a rage.
I call out to him again but he is so ashamed of my softness here—
as if they are his fault, my breasts, I know it. My hips
in worn blue cotton. My hair that fuzzes at my neck inviting breakage.
Broken already.
Everything in here is harder than I am, the tools' thick surfaces, the
    machines, chuffing,
that eat the bolts off tires, the dangle
of fan belts cluttered on the wall behind him, and nozzles like parts of
    his body
I mustn't see anymore—he is embarrassed for himself, so reduced. Not
for me, this is:
for himself and the others. For Jimmy
back in the office and Horace out front pumping gas, gabbing. For baby
    Fitz
who just last week married his pregnant sweetheart and she's already
guilty as I am, swelling up in secret, scaring the boy half to death. When
    I talk to my son
he hits a button and a silver car rises
and rises between us on a hard oiled stalk.
He keeps to the other side of it, poking
its underparts. He is the only man in the shop, of course,
who came out of such a delicate darkness as mine. The only one
who cried when they lifted him up from his bloody nest, lunging and
    gasping. As if
he was born cold as a wrench or a hammer, slicked shiny with motor
    grease.
As if I was ever
as fragile as he thinks I am today.

*

There was once another of us at the table. What
does my mother see when we sit now
shoulder to shoulder, Sam and me?

Sam remembers her, he says, but
only by the littlest things: how red and blue barrettes,
like gumballs, held her hair. The smell of her talcum
after the baths they took together. He doesn't know
what she was *like,* he says—she was too young
to be like anything.

Her name was Lacy, after a family of Irish
somewhere back on the tree. I always thought that was lacy,
like-a-doily, I'd picture her baby hands
in the holey, hand-shaped maple leaves flung down on the lawn,
eaten to the bare ribs. I'd lift a handful and look
through a tender crumbling leaf to nothing
on the other side. By then I knew
that's what she was: some strange and whispered nothing, and I—
had I come to take her place? But *I* was *me.*
It made no sense.

Mother didn't talk about her much, but I could see
her eyes fill sometimes, for no visible
reason. My mother had a mystery life I was jealous of,
a grief so large my being here could never replace it. Gone,
I learned well, and quick, and early,
was better than Right Here, spilling things,
disobeying, fighting with Sam until we got the palm
of our father's hand: Lacy, before she had words to object,
was delivered into perfection, a heavenly consolation
for not being real anymore, and every year
I grew past her baby picture (mouth like a Cheerio, a fountain of hair
     gushing
up through her head) I thought: Doomed. But I meant myself.
There was no glamour in it, living. Dead,
she stopped while she was still ahead, that innocent

favorite, I thought, which did me harm
while it did her—poor lacier than thou—
no earthly good.

*

Coming home late from work,
I stopped the car one long thirsty minute
on the hilltop near my father's meadow.

Something plunged and tossed in the center
like a show animal in a lit ring.

He threw his head, he shook it free of air,
his legs flung whichway. There were the antlers,
a forest of spring twigs that rose and dived,
dancing. *Singing,* for all I knew, glassed in.

I rolled my window down
knowing I'd lose him, and I did: he ducked
into nowhere. But I had that one glimpse,

didn't I, of the animal deep in
the animal? Of his freedom flaring

only a quick blink of light? I think spring
must be a crazy water animals drink.

*

When my mother took to her bed,
her face gone soft as a tea towel,
her voice the narrowest frying thread, we stood
and wept and prayed and fretted
that she not turn mortal on us,
she who had been invincible, as hard
and fast, as steady-burning, as ironwood.

But this was only practice,
a rehearsal for the real—at dawn

there she was at her breadboard, singing.
Was the spell for her only, to introduce
her slowly, a glimpse, to the mere idea of weakness?
Or was the brush of that shadow-wing
meant for the rest of us, so damnably helpless,

that angel springing open the coffin door
just long enough for a wind to cross her kitchen
and keep the bread from rising?

                    *

Not the inches around my waist,
no longer invisible under the right kind of pleats.
Not the way I improve my hair with this magic
potion. (*Always test before using. Do not use on brows.*
Just leave them to their fate,
those little stabs of silver you can't tweeze out.)

Not weariness or cramping thumbs,
or the doctor who used to say casually "At your age . . ." and dismiss
me, and now says darkly "At *your* age . . ." and orders tests.
It's joy. It's promises kept, not broken.
Joy. I know you don't believe me.

It's every happy milestone that looms
and passes: Chip brings home Michelle,
freckled and sweet, and, watching them together,
I face the truth still shocked, under my welcoming smile, my wedding
hairdo, that the woman in his life is not
his mother.

Nan brings home from school
no man but a passion for rocks: Who would try
to daunt her? She doesn't climb them, she
collects them in a sack, carries it lightly, my light-limbed daughter,
as if it were filled with mushrooms, learns mouth-breaking names
I can't pronounce, and now she's off
to a deep ravine in Arizona to pin
some weighty mystery down. I think

I envy her—not the gray basalt in a jagged hunk,
only the passion, the freedom to
care, to go, for its own sweet sake.
"*Relationships* aren't everything," she says,
and I can see by the way she rolls her eyes
what she thinks of me.

But I said it was the milestones: how each time
something happens that we have always expected—
events tolling like bells, never quite surprising—
what can I think of but the final
stone to come, the day they tell us will also arrive,
sooner, later, but no way not arrive? They haven't lied
yet—we'd better believe them.

Each good day says This is what it is to live.
As you are now, so once was I.
Die, says the wedding day, *Die,* says the live birth.
Prepare yourself and follow me. And I do, I do,
now more than ever, every year, prepare.
A promise is a promise, it's only fair.
We raise a toast—"To Chip and Michelle then, cheers!"
The aftertaste of this sweet champagne is bitter.
No one would guess I know that,
seeing me smiling here.

ANOTHER KIND OF TRAVEL

While you run all over the world looking for something
    you will never find,
I stay at home and travel all over Judevine Mountain.
    I clamber up the brooks
and into the caves, from the highest to the lowest,
    in the dark and
in the light, I go to places where I've never been and
    all of this within
what seems familiar, old and new, comfortable and
    dangerous, all
right here at home. And every evening when I get back
    to my house and while
I eat my rice and vegetables I look out at the slopes
    of Judevine Mountain
where I've just been and I ponder that day's handful
    of little discoveries,
I call them poems, that have come to me by
    never leaving home.

NORTH IS NOWHERE

*The solitude of the mountain is so great
that not even the poet himself is present.*
              — OCTAVIO PAZ

North is nowhere, nihil, emptiness and Judevine Mountain is north.
Come to Judevine Mountain and step into oblivion. Lose yourself

in this remote and lonely wilderness. There is no mirror here, no way
to tell where you might end, the others begin. Here you are no one,

only one—with everyone. Come to Judevine Mountain and find out
who you are. Come to Judevine Mountain and disappear.

QUIET AND SELDOM SEEN

Less than four hours southeast to downtown Boston,
less than three northwest to Montreal, less than seven

south to New York City, yet prowling through the mists
among the cliffs on Judevine Mountain are deer and bear,

moose and some say the reclusive catamount, the panther.
I prowl here too, among these beasts and all the others,

all of us, by nature, quiet and seldom seen together here
in our wilderness surrounded by that world of yours.

SPRING CLEANING

Mrs. O'Finnicky flounces her dust
ruffles, her mind bent on spring. All winter
she has endured the turgid company
of tchotchkes and assorted bric-a-brac,
of knickknacks worn by constant polishing
until her very need to keep them fresh
has left them faded as her own spent cells;
and yet these souvenirs remind her less
of anything she was than what she's not.
She cleans a reproduction from the MET
of an Egyptian hippopotamus,
then lifts a terracotta camel sent
by a daughter on a middle eastern tour—
how many years ago? Dust clings to it
as though it still lived on the *badiya*.
She pauses, briefly, fancying herself
a nomad, wandering across a plain
of twisted outcroppings of sun-bleached rock.
She feels a sudden faint, sweet twinge of thirst.
An empty water skin slaps at her thigh.
But somewhere on ahead the lush pastels
of a greeting card mark what ought to be
a palpable oasis, so she goads
her camel through the maze of monuments,
on toward the verdant show. And there she finds
only a canyon's vertical, blank walls
to echo back her emptiness. She counts
the years since either daughter visited.
She thought she had outgrown that loss. But still
her reverie wells up like a bruise; how
she'd fete them with corn-fed, yearling calf, spring
chicken, camel's milk koumiss, the thick fat
dripping and crackling on her heart's banked coals.

STOCK

        And Hope
was never happier than when her stock-
in-trade lay spread out all around her: old
bones feathered with stray wisps of meat; a cheese-
cloth sack of gizzards, slightly over-ripe;
two onions sprouting slow green horns like snails;
the stiff, bent back of a spinster chicken, pin
feathers still clinging to the shawl of skin
that hung in folds around its neck; a rib
of wilted celery; and thyme enough,
of course, to savor everything.
        Her sink,
she often thought, was like a riverbank
beside which she would stand and idly dream
of distant freshets whose cold, chuckling rills
sluiced down a stone-strewn, mountain bed to feed
the waterfall that tumbled from her tap.
She dropped some parsley in a tributary
runnel whose placid backwaters were dammed
off from the larger current by a rock-
like mass of moss-draped giblets she had found,
weeks past their prime, inside the fridge.
        Upstairs,
her mother offered an opinion of
the longish silence with an eloquent
rap of her cane against the antique headboard.
Like her, it came from old New England stock,
and it, too, showed its age—the finish worn
in patches where her pillow rubbed year in
and out until the wood showed through like sores
that damasked her back and legs. Yet neither oak
nor flesh relented, as if each were bound
to wear the other into dust.
        Thank God
for her disposal, which, though temperamental,
most often wolfed down anything, unlike,
she mused, her mother, who was known to pray

to God for strength while trying to choke down
her daughter's culinary wanderings.
At one point or another she had claimed
that everything but steak broiled half to death,
roast chicken, or plain stock would kill her, but
thus far, her daughter noted, nothing had.
For which she hastily gave thanks.
                   To dress
the old girl for a meal took twice as long
as dressing anything she deigned to eat.
To less effect, she'd be the first to say.
Yet she insisted on the ritual,
which made for more than one cold, silent meal.
But both knew if not this, some other fault
would raise its ugly and unfilial head.
Her voice rose like a hand to smack her child:
She might as well have fed it to the cat
for all the good this supper did.
                   Yet eat
they must, and often, made more often by
how well they know each other's gustatory
smacks and gurgles. Every gasp and fart
sighs like a last breath from the mother, full
of . . . what? Reproach? Her spoon clanks sullenly
in her empty bowl. Her child refills it with
a broth that smells somehow of sweet and sour,
though seasoned with no spice but thyme. Starving
for something thick and rich as loam, she eats,
staving off death, beyond all hope.

NEW ENGLAND GHAZAL

In the beginning were the Words of God, disguised as stones:
like hard, black pupils dropped into the faithful's eyes, these stones.

Waves hunched in worship shake the granite shore beneath my feet
as once it shuddered under the soles that colonized these stones.

Salt of the earth, they said, "Let nothing grow upon this spot
till hell silts over. Let them lie among blowflies and stones."

No schist for me, no strata resurrected from dead tongues.
I'll cleave to coal and shale and strive to anglicize the stones.

Cursing a blue streak when his plow beached on a granite spur,
the farmer wiped his brow, letting his sweat baptize these stones.

"Fuck you, you fucking fucker," froths a four foot gradeschool kid,
thrilled to outdo his friends, who've grown curt, coarse, streetwise, like
                                                                               stones.

Praise limestone. Mouth a marble chip. Haunt dikes, tors, sills, and crags.
In drought, clay sheathes its softer self and identifies with stones.

Such meditation on the inner life: the CAT scan's Ommm;
unearthly images of what metastasized as stones.

Who doesn't long to blame someone for their infirmities?
I turn to God and nature, but their alibis are stones.

The Jackal sings his privy business to the world at large.
Hungry, unfit to kill, he grumbles lullabies to stones.

NOCTURNE

I discover I'm missing. I never meant to go.
The street looks soft beneath a lamppost.

Night moves slowly in its yellow light.
Blackbirds locate each other with questions.

A girl on the corner continues to wave.
She no longer sees her friend.

I notice the back of a head in a window,
a shoulder turning slightly.

Surely someone has seen me.
Birds watch from the underside of trees.

Somewhere an infant cries and can't explain;
how can it say where the pain is?

I no longer hear the child, just the quiet
of a passing car and one or two bird calls:

Here you are. Where are you?
And *Where have I gone? I meant to go home.*

THE PLAYGROUND

A child has left her toy behind,
a small blue bear. Empathy is deadly,
but you look her in the eye.
Sit on the steps now
where no one can see you,
almost no one knows it's you.

We're so alone, we hardly know ourselves,
to whom our hands belong.
Each day stings. And so we're shy
with strangers, their disappearing faces.
Love is sad like laughter.
I will be your friend from childhood.

Listen—a mother whispers
in her child's hurt ear:
Can you hear me? she says,
What am I saying?
An orange rolls away from a lunch box
past a man's lost glove, its empty fingers.

A child chalked her outline
on the pavement. She drew a line
around her head and half her shoulder,
switching hands to draw the rest.
You keep going back
but you can't find her.

You were four years old
in your little dress, you said:
I have something to tell you.
Kindness was a way
of saying please don't die,
the way children try
to save each other daily.
That was only part of our lives.

This morning, your thumbprint
on the subway window
was a hummingbird's wing. I saw it.
A conductor said: *Make sure
you takes what's yours.*
Now the softness all around us is the air.

Here are our hands. Our hands
are here, I promise. There's strength
in our fingers to keep things.

The bicyclist behind you
says: *Don't be afraid.*
Listen to his trailing bell.
This friend is stopping near you.

Your hand inside his hand
turns towards him and away
and towards him. Awkwardness is honesty.
We'll find our families in strangers' faces.
Soft voices make us cry.

LONESOME *IS A CURIOUS WORD*

You keep entering empty cities.
Birds fly out of open doors.

Please: appear in every window;
whisper to the leafless trees.

Consider your syllables: *lonesome* is softer
than *lonely,* more melodious than *alone*.

Walk from room to room.
Wade through flooded basements.

Inside, the air is yellow.
Outside, the air is full of wings.

Listen—locusts buzz despite the sparrows.
you must murmur human sounds:

slow litanies to the sidewalks, to the gray
and narrow streets; mumble lists at least,

if you feel too shy to scream.
Whisper to abandoned buses:

lonesome, lonely, alone,
to the stopped and darkened cars.

Whisper to the deep horizon,
to the trees, the hovering wings.

Instinct makes the insects sing,
and so they find each other.

FALLING WATER

Wherever it commences perhaps as random
    raindrop tapping on a leaf and tumbling
        into a tea-stained mosscup

it helplessly inquires after
    lower levels whether seeping
        darkly through silt

and marl to enlarge an imprisoned
    aquifer shortcut or taking its chances to trickle
        out through a slit of clay to join its first

brook and amble off into the yielding
    soft-shouldered marsh past fat roots of
        lilies to linger among the slick fronds

of algae paddled by ducks pierced by
    pickerel to hurry itself and
        whisk into the outlet that will boil it

along a streambed grid of gravel toward another
    stairstep of idleness the lax
        lake spritzed with yawning sun

there to seek a breach to tip and hurtle
    into torrent and the great meander
        that will sweep it slow and away out

and empty into the broad salt
    sleep that will cradle it until
        the sun siphons it again
        to knit into more rain.

FARMER AND WIFE

sleep a lot, winters. (Less so
    as spring shoves daylight toward
        its limits and birdly

orchestras intensify dawn's clamor.)
    Weeding, watering, milking, and emergency
        adjustments to fencewire and balers

flicker through our waking, silent winter nights.
    Dark seasons stifle us, insist that
        we recalculate our chances.

Our children, near grown, have been dancing to
    distant music, flagellations of desire
        manipulated by worldwide "talent agents."

Our neighbors have concentrated on trading up, selling out
    to the enticements of Real Estate
        and their intensifying need for

quick-acting contraptions. The black soil of
    our acreage drinks deeper and deeper from
        sinister supplies.

Although our harvests bluntly persist, yielding
    sweet forage as well as
        burdock, in our winter sleep

we can hear the future
    inching up nightly,
        into its own, into
        the sure day of exile.

HOMAGE TO ROBERT FROST

He tramped flatfoot past
   the alders, over a stunted brook
      into the thin birches

at the back, up plank steps into
   the dark cabin, shuffled to the
      Morris chair and sat. Drew

the writing-board across his lap, uncapped
   his broad-nibbed pen, and pondered
      the gestures of conferring,

onto the foolscap, his choice from among
   the sounds that had been whirling
      in his head as he walked,

satellites to a gravity that had
   for weeks occupied his mind.
      Neither he nor anyone

could tell you exactly
   by what authority
      the words happened to alight—

to be tested, to be kept or dismissed. But
   here they lie now, at ease,
      carrying their fresh-picked

burdens of vowel and consonant,
   prefix and conjugation, freed at last to radiate
      stark terror, suspicious joy,
      the chromatics of grief.

LIKE NO OTHER

As I followed my road
  the atmosphere altered
    into a susurrus under the pines

and took shape in the lightfoot
  lope of a rapt fox
    a red and ragged vixen

absorbed in her intentions
  taking no notice that
    I was about to cross

her path. Closing fast
  catlike or rather foxlike
    in concentration she

pursued a faint
  trail across the road
    under a fallen tree

toward the kits in her lair
  coming from the lake
    her belly full of water

nose half lowered
  to where
    deer showed. The ground

reeked with the odors
  of forest traffic
    as her track led
      away into the woods.

A WAKE ON LAKE CHAMPLAIN

As an F-16 unzips the sky
a white-sailed yacht races in
like a surrendering rider
from the plains of the lake & a boy
conjures doves with a piece of cake.

Gas pumps plug their fingers in their ears.
You can hardly hear a child start to cry.
Her father fails to rock her still.
Afterwards he remarks this jet is guarding
Plattsburgh Nuclear Base or on border drill.

Now she's mesmerized by a duck & drake
teaching paddling, oblivious fledgling
how to play follow-the-leader.
A peace sign spreads in their wake.

VERMONT AISLING

Vermont was like a wooer
whose attraction
you shut out, preoccupied
with a lifelong crush

But lately
you've been taken
with this place,
especially since

snow covers
any resemblance
to that other one
& its perpetual row,

stilled beneath
the snow's silence.
May it snow for ever
& for ever now.

A poem in the Irish tradition in which Ireland is a woman.

THE GREAT SHIP

Later tonight
it's to turn cold, the old sudden sharp
    iceberg cold of New England.
Crickets, cicadas, grasshoppers and frogs
    play away.
What their songs, their wing-music is saying
    I can't say,
except they must know already that the ice
    has gashed a gaping hole
in the hull of the Indian summer and they
    are the quartet
that comes out on deck and plays away
    as the great ship goes down.
We are listening quietly from our deck's lifeboat.
    Play on
brave, noble souls. Play on. *Nearer my God to
    thee. Nearer to thee.*

AMERICAN SUBLIME

Closing time at the Athenaeum,
but this visitor bat
(who knows how he got in)
seems intent on staying the night;
our waving arms, a rolled Times,
the janitor's broom haven't phased him a bit.

In flits and starts he swoops
in crazy eights from cornice to
pilaster, chandelier to book-
shelf top, finial to plaster-
work to pediment. He seems
especially to like the vast

painting he skims like a pond,
a Bierstadt prospect of Yosemite,
billboard for immensity. The painter's
out to correct our sense of scale:
grandeur meant not to diminish
but enlarge, as the eye hurries

up that cleft dome of rock
to hazy light, light made material,
crown of glory, a suffused
atmosphere intended to mean
intensely. Our adventurer
doesn't stop to look, careening

above this antique ad for fresh air
as though he owned it,
and these books and music stands
and brass easels which display
last century's genre paintings
leaning back, labeled, heavily framed,

What's more out of date, nature
or the representation of it?
A velvet dust-rag wing
brushes canvas, granite dome,
the vanished vastness,
then rests a beat on that bust of

—Emerson? And now we
visitors, though we've all enjoyed
the unexpected fluttery show,
give up. Time to go home.
Where did we park? Dim the lamps.
Last glance: bat and Bierstadt

all in the dark. Nothing. No,
there he is! Flying, just visible
in the faint signal of the exit sign:
our little hero circumambulating still
the gloss of oil, the polished pools
and waterfall, our rocks and rills.

TIME ON MAIN

   The Masonic Temple—white clapboard,
columns straight from some Egyptian opera set—
   began in resolution, but settled
to something jaunty, accommodating time.
   The stacked, half-cocked steeple's clock
permanently stopped at quarter past twelve.
   Noon? Midnight? Whatever;
it has two accurate moments,
   a kind of achievement,
after all these years. The living Masons
   must be few, and wise,
here in the plain north, to keep
   a staunch white meeting house
to disguise their treasury
   of costume: luscious get-ups,

staffs and turbans and robes,
  the ritual fabrics of dream.
Three steeples rise from Main Street's sleep
  cloudward (each of them pointless):
the Mason's frame homage to Luxor,
  the congregationalist's dour stack,
and this: above arched windows
  inscribed, in marbled glass,
LOOK UP, a little Delphi's hung
  against the sky, twelve columns
squared around an open shaft
  of pure New England air.

Then a spate of retail, equally dreamy:
  a new trinket shoppe,
Gifts for the Soul. Black block letters
  —BRAD'S HOUSE OF TIME—
ring a neon clock. In the cemetery,
  a hillock where two routes
converge, flat slate markers lean
  in rows, delicately inscribed:
urns and winged skulls, willows
  bent in perennial grief.
Answered, somehow, by one man's
  stone engraved in cursive
with a motto and farewell:
  It's all right. Time,
I'd like to think he meant,
  his hour, and ours, here in Egypt,
Vermont, Greece. Imagine
  thinking the passage of time
all right! A proposition this town
  considers still, all night long,
the moon a chill frazzle
  in the rapids by the shut-down
mill, caught like Main
  in one continuous dream,
riddled with history, and outside it,
  sending these spires up
into October, year after year,
  at quarter past the hour.

BLEEDING HEART

Abruptly it unblossoms
and disappears, though among
the first of the spring—

the tulips worn out with blooming
after only the second year, daffodils
inexplicably nothing

but a vigor of leaves, a frailty
of azaleas—among the first of the spring
the short-lived Bleeding Heart

is certain, I can count on it.
A white variety bleeds
a tranquil pink, but this old plant

came with my garden, how old
I can't guess, but it's always been here,
or at least as long as I've been here,

not white, but scarlet,
sometimes a dull claret, in either case
bleeding one creamy drop, its languorous

long sprays drooping
over the patch of garden
that will in a few weeks

lie deep in the barren
shadows of the peonies.

RAKING THE LEAVES

For the second year in a row
I've let things go, neglected the leaves: the golden
platter-sized leaves the maples discarded
all through golden October, that layered themselves
to a four weeks' deepness, the days and long nights of October
dense with the soft undertones of their falling.
Another year over, another year,
and confronting accumulation, I hang back
from raking the leaves, inert beyond
all inertia, until with the late rains they've thickened
and swollen, grown sodden and thick—I've assumed the guilt,
excused myself from the task for the sake of my hands, hips,
knees, also from sheer laziness, and yet
all winter accused myself, foreseeing the labor
of raking the leaves, heavy and wet,
dreaded the work as I dreaded
the thought of it. Now, unwilling
I've brought myself to it and found,
this warm, sunny day in mid–April, crocuses
blooming and in the few beds of the garden

not smothered in leaves thrust on thrust
of lily and peony—found
the first layers soft with the first
sun of the year one might call truly warm,

wet, soft, almost to crumbling,
already commencing the laborious turn
toward mold, though still
with something left of the gold of the down-

drifting light they were; and then
a few inches down I come to the frost,
the durable cold at the final layer. Suddenly
there's a sense of bulb and rhizome, root,
runner and seed reclaiming themselves, thrust on thrust

into the crumbling cold of the leaves, a great
discharge of green light everywhere
all the luxuriant frills of the gardens

folding out from themselves.
In the final days of October
let all who doubt the resolve of accumulation,
who all their lives have wanted the world

neatened and cleaned and bared to the sharp
definitions of boundaries, despair. Here, under the leaves,
even stone is fragrant, the gardens
breathe underfoot. The chill

cover of leaves bears down on the gardens, the gardens
bear back. I honor the leaves
that bury my garden, surprise myself to find that I love
the gorgeous debris, whatever requires removal. Disheveled

and breathless with labor, I swipe at the frozen leaves, I foresee
I'm destined to live a long life, letting things go.

PERENNIALS

These perennials
unweeded, unthinned,
and left to go wild,

have won out this year,
have strangled everything
that shouldn't be here.

The earth is choked with growth!
Long ago I had foreseen
this bright day, this empty place.

Well, all to the good. Let the house plants
burst their pots, let them make it
or not. Let the garden grow

and seed and grow and seed
dry up, collapse under the fall
leaves, let the composts

commence their rich
fever, let the dead leaves
of the geraniums go

unpicked, let pansies seed,
let leaves and petals blow
into the neighbor's yard

and make colorful drifts
at the roots of his fences.
Nor will I prune the grape vine.

MOVING FROM WILLISTON

One gets used to everything
it's painful to recognize
the skill we have at it

what we really desire
is to be alive in somebody's eyes
we line up to be remembered

in the bedroom when the bed
is taken out, there
is the old floor showing

the honey-brown of the old pine boards
in the shape of the bed
surrounded by a glossy field, a garden plot

of green-going-to-black
one of the spaces
to be dispensed with, disposed

of utterly, and helpless
against being returned to
to walk through the dark doors

and find we are not in
has to be watched out for,
there are rules for this kind of thing,

severe penalties once we exceed the
boundaries of the general unhappiness
whatever is lost

or out of place of the places
we lived in—I don't mean
the ordinary landscapes

of a house, lightfall
in a room, or the peculiar echoes
of closets, earth smell

of basements, water stains shaded
and contoured to the shapes
of a woman's face, a map,

or nothing but a water stain . . . I don't mean
these things, they
are recoverable, they insist

on their availability
I mean everything
closed off from view

and one day released
to the dumb lament—
make it so that I can say it

plainly if not simply
let them go down with me,
keep me faithful to the rage of the displaced.

STORM

Outside the snow comes rolling in
from the flats of Quebec. It's the flat push
on things I fear. The north glass
rattles and bulges, the big poplar's

ready to fall, and crush the house, the bedroom
in a dust of rafters, bat dung, explosions
of plaster, cow hair, mineral wool, a rat's bones,
and the wires singing with fire in the dark,

snapping, coiling and uncoiling in the dark.
Whenever the wind bears strongly
from Riviere de Loupe onto the north face
of the house and wakes me to the midmost

hollow of the room, when the last of the sky
hurtles away, and dogs howl
in all the kitchens of the town,
and the breaths of sleeping citizens

spill down the black pitches of their stairwells.
I think, locked in the windbreak box, what
if the trees fall, and I never sleep again? Around me

the house in joist and rafter sings out loud.

COUNTRY

Tables, chairs, a used refrigerator in a thicket
Of zinnias; a woman lifting a window blind;
A man crippled with fat who waves hello,
His dog on a short chain prowling in front
Of his angry shed, the fur unkempt and bearding,
Fervent as Rasputin to wrench free
And get to a new voice and a stranger's scent,
The garden primeval
With snails, wrung with yesterday's rain;

And the tire gardens, the pink & yellow rubber
Ringing the geraniums; the established names on the mailboxes
And gravestones weathering the rich light;
And the smell of old lilacs; the tin advertisements
For farm machinery rusting on the milk houses;
The lines of light between planks
Crookedly spaced; wasps' nests; starlings';
The surveyor's orange flags; the wrecked autos
Like specialty stores in a fenced lot;

And the auction block, the brisk rhythm
Of selling—going, gone—it is a journey
They no longer can keep ahead of, as under a tent
A revivalist and congregation melt
Into one large droning; or it is a big top,
The women tidying the trailers, tidying the junk,
With *Lonesome Road* on the radio, the men drinking beer
Around the clock, revving their engines,
And the mutt at leash end crashing left and right.

FLICKER

"Beauty is for amateurs"

Chisel-billed, eye cerulean, with a crimson nuchal patch,
flicker lay on the ground, still-warm, and went on aging:
intricate, stricken watch, pear in a dessicating wind.

I brought it home and began with the box of watercolors
to wash the eye with milk for the clouds and sky it fell from,
then dragged my partly dried brush over the rough paper surface

for true textures on the wings, imagining old orchards, umber and sienna,
where I'd seen the undulating flight of loose flocks. I studied
the yellow undertail, then daubed with the colored water

along the gray and dun stripes. As for my pulse, I felt for temperament—
for gravestone, for shadow—to affect the utter silence after a long, long day
of call, *whurdle, peah,* drum, and *wicka.* Then I blotted and scraped the
     throat.

I saw dusk falling like a comment on each detail
that led to it and gradually was lost and leaving.
A hint of song must be caught, a clarity of neither light nor memory,

and it must be in the physical form of the flicker
and the orchard where the wind makes a soft racket—song that breaks the
     learned heart.

I stared and stared by lamplight, stroking the white,
thinking sour-gum, dogwood, poison ivy berry, river mist, imagining the
     free side of the hills,
when a bead of liquid formed in the flicker's beak and pooled on my desk.

My evasions went up in smoke. With colors, tones, casements,
and stars with exact names, who could but feign the moments
once lived that will never be lived again?

Who has a home in this good world and doesn't yearn?
I do. It's mine. I do.

WINTER POEM

Far past the broken wall, slashed stumps,
homeward or homeless, the black birds
in long purple streaking cling
to the undefinable bulge of the world.

And again I am in winter,
walking across the bronzed marshes
where as a child I went alone to skate.

The branches and hedges held a strange transparency,
as though, at the fall of leaf,
a wall of green twilight reared against them;
and the pond accrued a green and stony glow.

The log on the edge of the pond,
the snow-covered rocks, and the frightened birds
seemed as much laden with deep breath as myself—

the soft thudding sound as I tromped
through the green twilight and the snow
enriched with deer-fall, quill, the sunk solids
of the earthbound.

                        I skated easily,
a part of winter, unknowing, like Brueghel's skaters,
black comedians who seem in their blackness

to be keeping watch over the whiteness of space;
like magpies; all of us dipping our wings
in the green twilight, verging
on the vacancy in which we have no place.

EEL SPEARING

Just before dawn a woman and boy have come
to the river, water all astir, boat bobbing
and softly slapping, and soon she is leaning forward

while he holds steady the boat. Where prickling brown
meets smooth shining brown in eddies, they watch
for the sinuous shadow of the eel beside a sunken rock.

The boy's face suffuses with a quiet glow,
and soon the breaking day will catch him, and us,
whose imaginations strain after the shape in the water,

in its purples and yellows—in a time made simple
by the motion of the waves rocking, filling in
the small depressions in the river bank, smoothing,

mixing and dissolving clots of earth. If any
are thirsty, they can cup hands and drink. For now
we all are looking into the dark stream and the darker

pools—under a spell, so when darning needles
and water walkers hop, then are flying, whichever
of them falling first falling to the frog who stirred

them up, we only see eel. The boat rocks,
the water almost opaque but for sun through alders
glancing off the crumpled surface in one breath

of wind, then sinking a foot or more, and it is
promise, tone, direction, regret, and love.
This is the power of their faces, the woman's

and the boy's, and of the eyes, vivid, hunting
in the river waters—seemingly so composed and eternal—
for what will satisfy, if only it can be found.

THE CHANGE

The wife has painted the bedroom floor, and tonight
they are downstairs in the study, in the pull-out bed
next to the sliding glass door. Beyond the deck
and back lawn their land climbs to a wood
and then a meadow. The world is awash in moonlight
so that from the clear dark cloud of the pear tree
plainly hangs the rope, still, where her boys
swung and laughed and landed, in those early days.
With her sleeping husband she lies in the bed and sees
the smoothed, long-shadowed moonlit land they own,
the room, even, full of the quiet glamor
that falls across the book shelves and the table,
out across the blankets and the floor
and deck and lawn and up into the trees
like a dream of gardens and assurances
well-painted and alive.
                              And then a cry
floats to her from out of the night somewhere,
rising cold in the glassed-out shining wind
a long moment, a thin bleating baby call
a rabbit makes when caught by a cat or a fox,
makes once, one time, only that once.

THE HILL

In my Ford, on a dirt path
above our glittering town,
having no secrets we finally talked of death,
rejecting burial yet agreeing that
if they coffined us together hand-in-hand,
love in some dark way would have no end.

We watched the lights below and kissed, poor hearts
together in a fiction of our lives. The sky
turned silver gray, and through the window came
the twitter of an early morning bird
to send us to our houses and our names
estranged on stones a thousand towns apart.

HORSESHOE CONTEST

East Woodstock, Connecticut
Fourth of July

After the parade
of tractors and fire trucks,
old cars and makeshift floats,
after speeches by
the minister and selectman,
after the cakewalk and hayrides
and children's games
are over and the cornet band
has packed up its instruments
and left the gazebo,
the crowd on the town
green begins to gather
around the horseshoe pit
where a tournament
has been going on all day
and is now down
to the four or five
best players—the same ones
every year, these old guys
who, beneath their feigned
insouciance, care about this
more than anything.
The stakes are high:
their name on a plaque,
their pride, their whole idea
of who they are,
held onto since high school
when they played football
or ran track—something
unchanging at their core,
small but of a certain heft.
Limber as gunslingers

preparing for a showdown,
they step up in pairs
to take their turns
pitching the iron shoes,
lofting these emblems
of luck with a skill
both deliberate and
offhand, landing ringer
after ringer, metal
clashing against metal,
while the others, those
who entered the contest
just for the hell of it
and who dropped out
hours ago, their throws
going wild or just
not good enough, stand
quietly at the sidelines,
watching with something close
to awe as their elders
stride with the casual
self-consciousness of heroes,
becoming young again
in the crowd's hush
and the flush of suspense,
elevated for these moments
like a horseshoe hanging
in the sunlit air
above them, above their lives
as dairymen and farmers,
their bodies moving
with a kind of knowledge
unknown to most of us
and too late for most of us
to learn—though I'd give
almost anything
to be able to do anything
that well.

NOT WRITTEN ON BIRCH BARK

When this afternoon
as I took my usual path
through fields and woods,
a patch of briars snatched
the poem from my hand,
I folded the paper up
and slipped it in my pocket,
trying for a while
to leave words behind.

But the world and the mind
work in funny ways,
for there on the path
ahead of me lay
a curled white page:
a strip of birch bark
whose native blankness
seemed to ask for words
but left nothing to say.

Jeffrey Harrison   55

FALSE CONSCIOUSNESS

for Elise

Perhaps your silence is just that—silence.
Two-year-old Ella spews her chewed carrot.
Six-year-old Natalie complains about fairness.
The dead kitty, Henry, remains alert
To whatever does or never occurs.
A spider dangles from its sticky thread.
Sawdust twilight increasingly obscures.
The sippy cup tumbles off the table's edge . . .

Hours came and passed unnoticed by us all.
The summer floods have scooped the dirt beneath
Us—excavating any sense of hope
And washing it down the Winooski Falls.
Calm breaths are like that folded leaf
Which breaks the foam of water's envelope.

DUCK BLIND

The mallards migrate south with Fall's fury.
They honk as if bad traffic lay ahead.
Their flight a V, that kind of wedge
That carves the cloudless air invisibly,
While hunters hunker down among the reeds
And blow their calls like horns to celebrate
Their tractors' final lap to cultivate
The fruit of summer heat's discharge of seeds.

The paranoid fly on, regrouping ranks,
As others, just as dumb, drop down their tails,
An act of trust, even submission, frail-
Ty so basic to landing on the banks.
The camouflaged men pump their guns with cracks.
The flat-billed heads explode off banded necks.

IDAHO ONCE

tried to metaphysically vaporize
me. I was driving, Moscow to Ketchum,
dirt roads through mountain passes for miles
and miles. The farther I went, the more real
those mountains became, the less real I was—
nameless, faceless guy steering a rental
car over roads not on the map. Next week,
half an hour northwest of Moscow, I lost
perspective again out on what they call
the *Palouse*. I was real enough, that strange
rolling landscape was, too, but I wasn't
there—or *any*where else for that matter.
I stopped the car and walked two football
fields' distance into one of those open
spaces. *I'm here! I'm here!* I shouted. Then
I jumped up and down like a dwarf having
a tantrum in a fairy tale. *Maybe
you are, maybe you're not,* whispered
the sky, the dirt, even the air I breathed.
Unsettling—that's what it was. A settler
was what I wasn't. Some hours later,
crossing mountains I'd read about, I drove up
over a curve that opened the horizon,
and there was half the planet divided
by a river wider than the Dead Sea.
Oh, baby, I told what shards of myself
I could locate there in the car, *I think*
(which was very little comfort) *it's time
to fly east.* Before the grandest vista
I'll ever witness, what I wanted most
desperately was to trim the hedge and mow
the grass at Thirty-Four North Williams Street,
Burlington, Vermont   Oh Five Four Oh One.

GOT POWER?

"Out since Wednesday morning,"
sings a free weights man.
"Getting used to it now."

"Got it back right away,
but the phone's still out,"
blusters a tennis player.

We're tired of talking
stocks, telling the old
jokes. "Oh, baby, that ice storm

was something else,"
shouts the stairmaster
fanatic. The squash player

next row over greets
his buddy, the Cybex
circuit guy, with

"Got power, man?"
A racquetball player
cheerfully claims

he lost a hundred trees,
and a treadmill runner
brags of his impossible

driveway, when a huge,
hairy stranger, drenched
in sweat, steps out

of the sauna to announce,
"Hey guys, I figured
this out last night, talking

to my wife. The world's
totally screwed up,
and it's not our fault."

THE NATURE OF YEARNING

for Lindsey and Bess

I.

This Northern August swells with warmth
the garden would burst and a trout waits
beneath the moving river surface
he holds steady until the brown caddis
fly floats above him he plunges upward
breaks the silent water then slaps down fat
as deer that graze the flat meadows while slowly
as in a dream of shadows a black bear circles
beneath trees ten thousand shades of green.

II.

All changed now quickened the morning
air in September lifts the spirit high
as one perfect trumpet note still
this clarity this concerto suggests
the coming death of tomato vines also
cucumber broccoli corn beans peas yellow
squash cauliflower all vegetables dead
or dying we wait the swelling of pumpkins
the blood flame turning of delicate leaves.

III.

High down out of Canada the geese were flying
all day my wife said that far-off honking
sound makes you feel lonely the trees were pure
fire for two weeks but now the leaves have fallen
all purple and brown the woods resound with axes
while men cut logs the children home from school
go out for kindling the leaves crackle the blood

of the animals flows richer and a white tail doe
sniffs the air at dusk her smoky fawn now half grown.

IV.

Chop the caught turkey's neck catch the buck
deer in gunsights fire shots deep into his heart
sling up his carcass to a thick tree cut open
his belly and handle the bloody heat and stink
of his guts shoot doves partridge quail
pheasant and grouse shoot rabbits shoot quick
squirrels and walk the stubbled fields with meat
on your back for soon the snow comes and with it
the silence at night when the wind wants man flesh.

V.

White December the elegance of pine trees
in snow with voices rising in praise of Christ
the soft child of winter all Bach Fasch
and Handel cannot hold Jesus' swelling song
but now the trout takes no food the bass
sinks into the darkest pools of the river
the bear's blood slows while goose and duck
have long flown south and beside the house
snow deepens over logs stacked for the fire.

VI.

Ice ice the death of trees the wind strips them bare
it whips them into savage rooted dances branches
crack limbs are yanked off they fall and smatter
on the frozen ground fearing wind I tell my wife
don't stand by that window a pane might burst
this morning she found stiff on the crusty ice
a redpoll dead and light as dust in her hand she said
the sun has forgotten us the nights go on and on
the clouds flee and the wind howls all day long.

VII.

No meat in the house we cut holes in the ice
this February we fished for smelt and perch the ice

on the lake was two feet thick my wife thinks
the birds have left us forever only the rats thrive
they steal our corn and leave us just cobs and husks
rabbits are hard to track now but one the other day
sat in the field he was so cold I walked up and kicked
him before I shot the ice builds its kingdom
and holds against what fire we have left love.

VIII.

We long for warmth these days there is little sun
still no birds have flown north over our house
and I think this March no month for birth only
the wind has life no green anywhere the trees
are just bones they shiver and bend they want
loose from this earth yesterday we saw the grass
it was brown and dead as an old hide in daylight
the snow melts some but it freezes again at night
the ground is covered with brittle crusts of thin ice.

IX.

Oh the waters burst there are the timid green buds
delicate grass crocus and daffodil the waters
gather they flow out of the mountain the streams
wash off dead limbs and leaves the gentle rains
bring birth this air of April wakes even the animals
the spring birds have come back the trout leaps again
now the wind is a child the earth is sunlit a woman
walks outside this morning she is beautiful as the clear
sweet sound a man makes with his horn at his lips.

HOT WIND, PROVINCETOWN HARBOR

Even blowing over the water it burns,
   pin-pricks of sand in every gust, hot
      sting of sun in its touch. The boys are

throwing rocks at the boats—they can't
   reach them, they're throwing fireballs
      into the sun, heaving great black fistfuls

of the earth's dried magma into the blistering
   light, breaking the water upward. Their voices
      are like bright arrows launched upward,

then quickly falling back. The wind parts
   around them, around whatever is thrown
      forward, ahead of them into the distance.

Two young men on the beach are watching
   my son and his friend; holding hands,
      they pause and turn with a sweet attention,

an admiration which is not greed but sympathy,
   I think, a memory of childhood, though
      they see me watching their watching,

and stop and go on. The boys are loud
   and skinny as train tracks, the ladders
      of their ribs running upward—

wouldn't anyone find them beautiful,
   with their bird legs and their wild voices
      the wind takes up, how their skin turns

brown and they fall back into the water
and then rise up, making waterfalls?
I sit at the edge of the beach, high up

where the grass ends, almost invisible,
a mother alert for rocks and strangers,
for sand in the eye that flies on this

hot wind. My legs are brown and so strong
—I have walked thousands of miles on them
already, as slowly as needed. I am thirty

years ahead of these boys, moving away from them
without them noticing, past the next bend
of the harbor, down to where the two men

have stopped at the edge of the water.
They face into the wind as if against a wall.
The smaller one is dark and frail,

and when he coughs his shoulders shake.
He stands bent over at the waist, head down
as if sick or despairing. No—he is untying

a little boat; they are climbing into it
together, rowing out against the incoming tide,
into deeper water, clearing shore.

SEA-MEADOW

Dawn burns. The window
tips its lens into my eyes,
all space focused
in a star, rising. Below,
the tall grasses strain in wind,
all thrill and glitter,
their white tips
lapping over. A towel

shudders and beats on the line.
Only the roses are quiet,
half-open on the brown stems,
above the sun-blazed leaves,
their pink buds complex
and folded as scars.
What is it to say,
"meadow, meadow, wind?"
The white path of sand running
up to the beach and down.
Sea-meadow
where nothing grazes. Wild,
for nothing. Only the mouse
who runs along the ground
picking up fallen seeds,
keeping out of sight of the hawk.
I write this in the voice
of a woman whose heart is broken,
who wakes and watches her mind
struggle to run from what holds it,
restless movements
that do not touch the root.
She is not young.
She knows her life will be
the things that have happened,
and her feelings will not move,
merely shake and flare in the light.
I write in her mind, her life,
because I will never be
that person. Look at me—
I am grass; the wind moves
through me, flustering;
morning burns me down my spine.
Out of the sky
a hunter aims his eye
of fire and a door opens
to tear me out of time.
Look at me. I am not
the grass, I am the meadow.

THE ANGELS OF 1912 AND 1972

It is a long time since I flapped my wings,
a long time since I stood on the roof of my house
in Lawrence, Mass., or Michael's in No. Andover,
a little whiskey in one hand, the past slipping
through the other, a little closer to the heaven
of dreams, letting the autumn wind, or the spring
wind, or maybe just the invisible breath of some
woman lift me up. It is a long time since I have flown
like a swallow, or even the clumsy pigeon, into another
time, practicing miracles, dodging the branches
of lost words that cut against the sky,
and the rocks thrown by small boys, finding
the right nest under the eaves of some pastoral age
even the poets have forgotten, or fluttering
to a slow landing on some ledge above the buses
and simple walkers of this world. It is a long time.
  From where we stood I could see the steeple of the French
church. Further back, it was 1912, and I could almost
see the tenements of the French women who worked
the fabric mills, weaving the huge bolts of cloth,
weaving the deadly dust into their lungs.
They could hardly fly, these angels. I could
almost see them marching down Essex street and
Canal street to the J.P. Stevens mill, the Essex mills,
pushing against the police horses for two bitter years,
thousands of them, asking for bread and roses, asking
something for the body, something for the soul.
If I did not fly so far I could see my mother's father
years later, stumble to the same mills, nothing gained.
Or I could have looked ahead to this very year, and seen
Bob Houston and me standing on a roof in Bisbee, Arizona,
two desert sparrows flying blind against the night
once again, remembering the union workers herded
into boxcars and shipped from there into the desert

a few years after my French weavers flew down
Essex street. But it was 1972 and we still believed
we could stop the war with a rose, as if there were
only one war and not the dozens of little ones
with their nameless corpses scattered like pine cones.
It was 1972 and we stood on the roof like two angels
lamenting the news that John Berryman had leaned out
over the Washington Avenue bridge in Minneapolis,
flapped his broken wings, dropped to the banks below him.
I am a nuisance, he wrote, unable to find a rose for his soul.
We thought we could stand on that roof in 1972, two
Mercuries waiting to deliver his message to another time.
I should have seen what would happen. I should have seen
my own friend on his bridge, or the woman who could have
descended from one of those French weavers leaning
on the railing of the north canal in Lawrence because
all hope had flown away, or my own father starting
to forget my name that same year. If there is anything
I remember now, it is the way he looked at me in his
last year, wondering who I was, leaning back against
his own crushed wings, just a few years after he told me
to fight the draft, to take flight, or maybe he leaned
as if there was a word no one would ever speak
but which he knew I would believe in, that single word
I have been trying to say ever since, that means
whatever dream we are headed towards, for these
were the angels of 1912 and 1972, the ones we still
live with today, and when you love them, these swallows,
these desert sparrows, when you remember the lost fathers,
the soldiers, when you remember the poets and weavers,
when you bring your own love, the bread, the roses,—this is flying.

VILLANELLE OF THE CROWS

(Montpelier, Vt., January 1999)

Your shadow whispered into mine as into the inner ear of snow
though this morning I could dream we were never really there:
the Heart sometimes panics, stumbling to fly off with the crows.

Clouds breaking into crumbs, words blown away with the snow,
and the moon, your shadow's moon, a clove of garlic against despair—
and your shadow, too, losing its balance in the inner ear of snow.

Why does everything pretend only what the moon chooses to show?
Moonlight with its arm around your waist, moonlight of your hair—
but my dull Heart would tear Love's carrion, dive in with the crows.

Why is it that the snow never covers what we finally owe?
Why is the heart always stumbling around in the soul's cold cellars?
Why was I waiting, angry—or suddenly filled with the fear of snow?

I was wrong. Everything we do only hides another guilt, or sows
a guilt that blooms white like a knife whose glint blares
across the fields, or startles a smile that turns the color of crows.

I have been watching the few stars spin cobwebs of cloud that glow.
I should have stayed. Maybe Love is just the shotgun blast in the air.
Tonight the empty air whispers. I myself am the inner ear of snow.
The Heart freezes. Words crack. Your Love flies off with the crows.

NO FAULT LOVE

No one seeing the suspect, Richard Jackson, should ever
try to approach him. His description contains as many
contradictions as Proteus. The heart's cabdriver
reports that he has fled into tomorrow because he is so
tired of speaking about yesterday. If you do not
recognize his crime you are already an accomplice.
Don't even try looking for him where he grew up
in Lawrence, Mass. The whole town is burning.
The remarkable thing about tomorrow is that everything is
the opposite of today. The shadow that now stalks you
becomes your confessor. And it is true, desire never
loses its grip on tomorrow. But just because tomorrow
follows today does not necessarily mean that one thing
always follows another. The bullet that is heading
for your heart may never arrive, the plane floundering

towards earth may even pull up at the last minute,
given the ambiguities and uncertainties of tomorrow.
None of tomorrow's verbs can ever finish what they're doing.
Trees stand for anything. Stars, too, stand for anything.
The whole galaxy screams something that is soon forgotten.
So you can forget about the Bosnian bells with their
human tongues. The business of tomorrow is pulling up
the roots of sadness so that the three children
blown up in the speed factory in Boston—
what am I saying? We want to live as if our own bodies
were nests. But possibility opens like the palm of
a waving dictator. You can scale the ruins of heaven
in search of love and never find it. But if you find
Richard Jackson tomorrow, or even the day after,
approach with caution—his words are snares.
The horrible thing about tomorrow is that today is already
history. We don't even exist the way we exist.
Truth becomes a fixture. Love wakes in the keyholes.
I don't know what other clues to give you.
All the good souls have fallen from their nests.
By tomorrow, the scene of the crime will be forgotten.
But the heart, the heart's fingerprints are everywhere.

KEEP BACK THE DARK

November and the sun
grows sparse in the sky.
The last fly perches
on the white nose of Punchinella
made by my Venetian mask-maker
who is dying.

Soon the bare birches
will be wrapped in ice,
squirrels will steal seed
from the birds'
swinging larder,
deer will tiptoe
in search of sweet green leaves
and find none.
wild turkeys
will fly, fly
away from Thanksgiving.

The earth is God's book
but in our blindness,
we have obliterated letters
so we may say
God has abandoned us.
It is we
who are illiterate.

Unable to read
the runes of divinity
around us,
in love with the idea
of being orphans,
we scribble to bring back
the dead.

STARLING

Heard its drumming first downstairs:
no dream at all, a large bird loose
inside the room—an open flue.
It clatters, swoops the tilting house
and clears the lamps and loops somehow
to sanctuary, green—the turret
of the window bay a terror-
struck and echoing vitrine, whose
wilderness of hanging plants
swings sickeningly, wing-slammed, sley
on twisting thread, and plain-weave sash
struck hard, and birdlime everywhere;
it whites the map where he'll not land,
a veer of lost flight back and forth
from light to light—I duck, a scare-
crow, duck again and back away.
His beak, his breast, his wingbeats snare
across the glass like castanets
until I think the gimballed earth
itself begins to sway—

And I too down the chimney straight
into the ancient uncast net
of nightmare: tonight, again, *the punctured
greenhouse:* where, high and frail, a spun-
glass arboretum starts to vibrate,
touched, high up—a shard of chert
tic, enters slowly like a small
star-drill, drifts down, transects the humid
chamber so, to kiss a far wall
tic, exploding outward in a plume
of glass—and hear, an insect hum
inside the ear, the conch shell sounding
at the drum, where scimitars

of falling plate whir down and scythe
the dark and cooling space inside
the room, its delicate cloud forest
first laid bare, exposed for the first
time to the airless dark, to the steep
and penetrating light of stars,
where every green goes sepia,
goes brown, and consciousness whorls down
no lullaby, no dream, to sleep.

DRIVING SLEEPING PEOPLE

Home drive. High beams shearing bromegrass,
blackcaps, brambles by the roadside;
red stems siphon frozen ground
grown soft, a bruise beneath the smooth suede
winter peach that rolls across
the dashboard. Thaw through frost. We pass
warm pockets now and then of sweet
spring air. Mount Equinox, Ascutney,
far ahead, still bear the weight
of ice, the Champlain Glacier's skirt
drawn back—imagine ancient beasts
suspended high, great woolly mammoths
half a mile above us cast
in ice, in time, the moon a beat
of fine rice paper wings—
                              White moths
are streaming to my windscreen, tracers
through the night that lies across
the sleeping globe tonight like thick
volcanic glass. One diamond scores
it. Somewhere sunrise, somewhere crows
lift off their power lines like quarter
notes suspended echoing
in mind again—such dark and lithic
deaths as lie ahead, smooth bulbs,
the denser black-in-black, dark knots

embedded in the grain of night
we pass through like a blade. I close
my eyes to this, to all impalpable
danger, now. They sleep, a nest
of starlings pooled into their own
black shadows in the back seat, sightless
son and daughter stir a moment,
mutter nothing, sleep again.
Against the door, an empty dress,
my wife, asleep, her face a surface
clear as water catching light
as cars flash by—
                              And I see what,
see changing patterns on the skin,
the wheel, this road, the pale surf
of mountains cresting in the starlit
distance, sea behind, its pull
and seiche inside us still, the trick
of centuries. We've measured Thuban,
Kochab, Vega, gone; Polaris
shining in its geometric
steeple somewhere east of north—
I feel its fixture in the dome,
the needles turning at the wrist,
the wheel for one extended moment
steady in my hand. . . . By earthlight
I feel this, the peace of this,
of driving sleeping people home.

PLUME

In the orchard,
puffs, plumes,
odd gusts—
when suddenly
the trees toss up
their blooms at once:
white petals

chimney up
and braid together
in the sky
like sweet smoke
from the same flame —
so beautiful!
And still, a shame.

APPLES ON CHAMPLAIN

Oil-slick, slack shocks, ancient engine
smoking like a burning tire,
Augustus' old truck yaws and slews,
its leaf-springs limp these centuries
suspending apples, somehow pulls
the last hill past the bridge at Isle
La Motte. I hear the iron arches
groaning. Why not? Whole orchards
rattling, empty racks behind us,
emptied into grain sacks, piled
behind us — home ahead, we broach
the mile-long causeway cross from Grande Isle
back.
      A blue heron's motionless
in marsh grass to my right, and pole
and icepack at my left — one line,
two lanes, a roostertail of blue
exhaust, we part the cooling waters
of Champlain.
            The moon's a pool
of mercury. It's zero. Ice soon.
Steaming like a teacup, losing
heat, the lake is tossing clouds up
all around the truck; and tucked
so in its fragile ribcage creel,
the cold heart *thump* accordions
to keep alive, and fills, as apples

interrupt this landscape's black-
on-grey like heartbeats full of blood,
strung beads, a life of little suns
gone rolling down the press and sump
of memory and changing form
as *thump,* horizon groans and ladles
light, and the real sun comes up,
sudden, weightless, warm.

TREES

I would leave by the back door
and make my way to the woods, on paths
I thought were trails of the Wampanoags,
paths at that hour still woven over
with scaly, cobwebby stuff
that had dew under it and dew on top.
I pressed myself to a white oak
and climbed. On the way up gravity
seemed to start pulling me from above.
At the top of this somnolent fountaining
of trunk, boughs, branches, twigs, leaf-splashes,
all of it tinned with the industrial dust
of Pawtucket in Depression,
I gave my ape-cry.
I knew the oaks' sermon to us
has to do with their verticality,
and their muted budding and brilliant decay,
and their elasticity, and their suthering and creaking,
and now and then their dispersal at the top into birds.
But I knew it had to do even more
with this massive, stunting halt
and the 360° impetus to spill outward
and downward and hover above their twin
glooming open under the ground
—at Loon Lake I had seen this in visions.
Out of the hush and rustlings came
chirrups, whistlings, tremolos, hoots,
noises that seemed left-poking up
after some immense subtraction.
Tok-tok-tok-tok, as from somebody
nailing upholstery, started up nearby:
the bird with a bloodmark on the back
of his head clung, cutting with
steady strokes his cave of wormwood.

On another tree, a smaller bird,
in gray rags, put her rump
to the sky and walked headfirst
down the trunk toward the earth
and the earth under the earth.
Drops of rain plopped into my hair.
I looked up and bigger drops tapped
my lips and cheeks. Unlike the cat,
who loves climbing but not coming down,
I came swinging and sliding down
hanging by my knees on the last branch,
and, as if the tree were one bell
of an hourglass which had been taken up
and turned over while I was up in it
and just as I slid through set down hard,
I landed with a jounce. The drops
chuting earthward all around me
were bringing back a kind of time
that falls and does not fly.
The red-topped bird kept working in the rain.
I had seen my father stand most of a
day pushing and lifting
his handsaw. All hand tools, I thought,
were the trees' equals, working wood
no more easily than a woodpecker's auger.
I had not yet caught in the crosscut's
grunts and gasps the screams, in time
to come, of chainsaws, or in the steady
drudging *hunhs!* of the ripsaw the howls
of supersaws clear-cutting the mountainsides,
or in the *har-har* and handshake
of the developer the loud bellowing
and hard squeeze of tree harvesters; I had not
conceived its own pulverized
pulp being ripped out in an arc at the foot
of every tree, I had not witnessed
the imperceptible budge, the dryadic pop,
the slow tilt and accelerating topple,
the dry splintering crash of tree
after tree like the end of history.

And yet—as I walked—a scrub pine brushed
dust off my pants, a birch branch knocked
debris of bark from my shirt, a leaf-clump
of a white cedar seemed to reach down and,
as if to preempt the work of the hairbrush
ready to harrow its spiky bristles across
my brain-skin in the morning at the front door
on my way to Sunday school, smoothed my sodden hair.

THE EXCHANGE

The neophyte animal psychic
visits my barn at midday.
She is wearing for the occasion
aquamarine eyeliner
a sequined bow in her hair
and a slippery nylon jacket
my gelding loves to explore
with his delicate muzzle.

What do the horses, those thousand-
pound engines of passion and flight,
the horses, long my conspirators,
tell her, who's newly beguiled?
She says the old broodmare knows
how in the other life
I dined abroad with crows,
carrion my caviar.

She says the sloe-eyed fillies
know in the next I am meant
no more to eat flesh but simply
to pick grass, switch flies, and roll
as my horses roll after work
thudding down like a wagonload
of watermelons to tip
from side to side on the sand
scratching the struts of their backs.

And yes, I can feel the itch
ascending my spine as we
observe this ritual together,
something, she now confesses,
she's never witnessed before.
I tell her the ancient Hindus

moved by this scene, inferred
how their gods and demons, while
churning the ocean of milk
in order to make nectar, erred
and out of chaos brought forth
with dished profile, kind eye
and mane woven from many strands of silk
this magnificence, the horse.

THE POTATO SERMON

Exhumed at the end of the season
from their caverns of love, their loamy
collectives, the little red Norlands
here nibbled at, there split or malformed
turn up in blind budded clusters
smooth cheeked, delicate, sometimes
surrounding a massive progenitor
while the thick-skinned long-keeping
Kennebecs that at first pretend
to be tree roots or fossils or wrist bones
are rewards for the provident.

You must do this on your knees
switch hitting, with long pauses
closing your eyes as you tunnel
the better to focus on feeling.
The dirt that packs under your fingernails
forms ten grin lines as if you had clawed
through bricks of bitter chocolate.
It's an Easter egg hunt underground.

Once mounded up in the larder
there is starch for the orphan's belly
there is radiant heat for the hungry.
Go forth as if to partake in
night failing, day beginning.
Go forth. The task is simple.
Deliver the warty earth apple.

SKINNYDIPPING WITH WILLIAM WORDSWORTH

I lie by the pond *in utter nakedness*
thinking of you, Will, your epiphanies
of woodcock, raven, rills and craggy steeps,
the solace that seductive nature bore,
and how in my late teens I came to you
with other Radcliffe *pagans suckled in
a creed outworn,* declaiming whole swatches
of "Intimations" to each other.

Moist-eyed with reverence, lying about
the common room, rising to recite
Great God! I'd rather be . . . How else
redeem the first flush of experience?
How else create it again and again? *Not in
entire forgetfulness* I raise up my boyfriend,
a Harvard man who could outquote me
in his Groton elocutionary style.

Groping to unhook my bra he swore
poetry could change the world for the better.
The War was on. Was I to let him die
unfulfilled? Soon afterward we parted.
Years later, he a decorated vet,
I a part-time professor, signed the same
guest book in the Lakes country. Stunned
by coincidence we gingerly shared a room.

Ah, Will, high summer now; how many more
of these? *Fair seed-time had my soul,*
you sang; what seed-times still to come?
How I mistrust them, cheaters that will flame,
gutter and go out, like the scarlet tanager
who lights in the apple tree but will not stay.

Here at the pond, your *meadow, grove, and stream*
lodged in my head as tight as building blocks,
sun slants through translucent minnows, dragonflies
in paintbox colors couple in midair.
The fickle tanager flies over the tasseled field.
I lay your "Prelude" down under the willow.
My old gnarled body prepares to swim
to the other side.

       Come with me, Will.
Let us cross over sleek as otters,
each of us bobbing in the old-fashioned breaststroke,
each of us centered in our beloved Vales.

INVITING THE MOOSE: A VISION

Sumac thickets by the roadbed, either side,
spangled by snow and the big moon's light.
Deeper in, evergreens, taller, darker,
but still undark in that light, this weather.
And deeper yet, hardwoods that scatter and climb
 up Signal Mountain, which I climb down in a car, toward home.
 A saxophone keens on the tape machine—slow, sweet
 balladry, which seems just right.
I whisper, "What a night."

Twenty minutes east, my twelve-year-old son
composes a story in his upstairs room.
His two younger sisters are breathing, way down in slumber.
Downstairs, my wife eases split remnant lumber
into the stove for kindling,
 and then—nothing grave—she goes on thinking.
 In mind and fact, the world appears
 intact, to me at least, who am torn between here
and there, to me who fears

one set of pleasures may cancel another.
It's like the dilemma of any lover,
craving anticipation and, equally, consummation.
But who'd complain at such benign frustration?
Everything glows. The wayside drifts, for all their sand and salt,
 are gorgeous as they descend, like the fault-
 less bassward glissando of the horn
 as I glide by Kettle Pond.
Whenever the season is warm,

its open water invites the moose of our region.
And I? I summon a vision.
My knowledge, for all my years, remains slight:
Why, I wonder, tonight of all nights,

should I invite the moose as well?
  Antlerless in late winter, the bull
  precipitously vaults the righthand guardrail
  and comes to a standstill
before my automobile.

One of the daughters shifts in dream. Rolls over. Smiles.
My son's narrative, meanwhile,
proposes at its climax that goodness is a sword.
The saxophone and the sidemen find their resolving chord.
All might end right now, right here.
  My wife muses by her warming fire.
  There's no moose, of course, just hallucination,
  on no particular occasion,
on a flank of Signal Mountain.

  No moose at all. Just strange desire.

YOKED TOGETHER

The warden, cop, and vet all told me on the phone the coon must be
                                                          destroyed,
provided, like them, I possessed the means to do it, as for better or worse I
                                                          did.

He'd come up out of our woods and onto the porch and simply would not
                                                          scare.
He had stuff running out of his eyes, and skinny, tatterdemalion hair

and he probably had, therefore, rabies. Or maybe distemper. In any event,
surely something was wrong, and according to the doctor, my good
                                                          friend,

something abnormal enough it likely posed a not inconsiderable health
                                                          threat
to our family, our dogs, our property, and to other families and to other
                                                          pets,

and also to what he called "the wildlife community." By the time I got
done
searching for keys for the gun cabinet, he stood out there in the winter
garden,

where now and then he pawed at the wilted greens of a buried carrot,
pausing
now and then as well to lift one foot, and next the other, and looking

more than anything bewildered.   He reminded me of poor gone
Arthur,
the idiot from one town away: he and I used to split up wood together,

and he'd sort of do the same thing with his legs, and his eyes were also
ringed
with black. (He smoked a filthy corncob pipe, through which everything

must pass: milkweed, leaves of grass, cigars, cigarettes, chew—you name
it.)
I suppose I thought of him because he too was above all else bewildered.

He'd squint and scratch his head, as if he never completely understood
—no more, really, come to think of it after all these years, than I could—

why I'd show up at his shack every late August with the saw rig and the
maul
to help him fill his woodshed, which was no more than an empty pony-
stall.

I imagined using, precisely, a maul on this poor, disheveled, sickly beast,
because I didn't want my small daughters to hear me fire the shotgun blast

that would do him in. Yet I admit I was also afraid to get too close,
and I likewise must have supposed a bludgeoning would make an awful
mess,

and somehow it might have felt too much as though I'd brought a heavy
blade
down on baffled Arthur, the coon's human image, as I've already said.

The shotgun having been fired, the creature fell and huffed once. Then:

silence.

And I, no more than a dreary man of letters, as if my knee had jerked,

thought of myself at one end and Arthur at the other of a cropped white

birch,

and of a famous poet's phrase about things being "yoked together by

violence."

WELL, EVERYTHING

After the cancer got down in his bones, old Bill
didn't want much to kill—not even on the wing.
Still, he did have that crackerjack young bitch Pointer Belle,
just now getting round to her best, her prime-years savvy,

Wouldn't she be the wrong damned creature ever to waste?
Then Joey, of course. The kid. Yes, Joey, too.
(40-something, he was by now: "The kid," by Christ!
but there *is* a whole lot of difference: 40 and 60).

He'd take them out, he would, old Bill McCrae.
The birds were scarce, they were wicked scarce, compared,
even in the county's last cover lasting a day.
Then comes the end of that day, the end of that season,

when you'll see those cones, foot-long, all bluey-violet.
Toward night they jump right out from your shotgun's barrels.
Near dark, but by Jesus, Belle points and holds it solid.
It seemed like a gift, to someone, the way things happened,

because up flies not just one, but two big grouse
(or "brace" as his late true-Scot Uncle Belding put it,
pretending to be old school or something, high class,
instead of some millhand stiff, like any McCrae).

Joe pulls up the leftside barrel, straightaway
(at least the boy still uses a side-by-side,

not like those city nuts from the NRA,
the ones that call themselves "ballistics experts").

You talk about expert! Belle holds and holds, by God.
Joe misses his bird, no matter he's made of himself
a pretty fine shot. Belle holds. Bill whispers, *Well, good*.
The kid drops the harder one of the pair in the dirt.

And Bill, he says it again, *Well, good*. You see:
It comes to him right then that everyone here
that isn't dead as that bird is more or less happy
when everything draws to its close. And thinking so brings

to Bill an old but a kind of far-off commotion:
he thinks all this is just like going through
any old sort of repeated, familiar motion.
Then, goddamn-it-all, as if it has wings,

the Christly Crab flies right back in his mind.
It's been a good life. It has, oh yes, more or less . . .
(Here Baby! Here Belle! Here Darlin! Here Sweetheart! Here Child!)
So what's so different now? *Well, everything*.

NORTH-LOOKING ROOM

In a rarely entered attic
you force a balky door
to open a room made brilliant
by an orange tree whose branches bear

no fruit but maple leaves.
This is New England, after all.
    Though rippling foliage fills
the pane, the flush that tints the wall

will last a week or two, no more.

    *

And this concept, if consoling,
of a bright, unpeopled room
    lit solely by a tree
holds equally—for those whose days

    sidestep round the fear
that in the give-and-take of calls
    to answer, calls to make,
they lose the light most dim, most clear—

a reprimand no breeze can shake.

SLOW WORDS FOR SHOREHAM
AND THE APPLE BLOSSOM DERBY

All the runners and near-runners start
to stretch the night before, to push against
the nearest wall in their sleep, then bend over
clasping the back of their calves like swanning
ballerinas. Here in Shoreham's apple country,
the annual spring run begins again in the May
blossom of their minds. Back inside the year
these local running friends see the year go

off across a chalked-in starting line that starts
in a church parking lot and runs the falling
hills nearly five miles down to Lake Champlain
and the reversing Ticonderoga ferry. The race
organizers try to time the run to coincide
with when the millionth apple blossom breaks
open and the route is a safe paradise from
pollinating bees. History tells them the first

hill is the quiet killer, a quarter down
and three quarters up to the Revolutionary
cemetery overlooking the unblistered lake.
But then, as it is said at the marathon in mother
Boston, after Heartbreak Hill, it's all downhill
from there. In between the untimed meadows,
the saintly, dumbfounded Holstein cows each
year come more and more to look like Woody

Jackson's mindful paintings of them.
Down across the temporary finish line
to the only stone building nearby the water
holding its share of lead shot and blood—

which still runs over these bursting apple hills—
they run by and stop to remember who,
out of breath, shoeless and unnumbered,
lay down and finished before them.

FIRST SPRING

*"About Ten A Clocke we came into a deepe Valley full of Brush, Wood-gaile and Long
Grass, Through which we found little paths or tracks and there we saw a deere and found
springs of fresh water of which we were heartily glad and sat us downe and drunke our
first new england water with as much delight as ever we drunke drinks in all our lives—"*
—NOVEMBER 16, 1620, TRURO, MASSACHUSETTS

They must have heard surf breaking the sand
into coast, and dry from drinking the left-over
dust of the ship's kegs, they went searching
for new water, tramping through the Cape's woods
toward the salty sound that carried them here.
Everywhere the blood-seeking mosquito bore
its small transfusion and the green-headed deerfly
branded the backs of their necks and arms.
How could they stay, not being blood-drinkers,
not having found yet and aged a fermentable fruit
into a fruit wine that could help them forget

and remember the beauty and loneliness of crossing,
of being here beautiful and alone? Thinking of freedom,
or rather a different pain, they risked going thirsty,
living on what they could find to take the place
of water. Rightfully, they thought of deer bending
to drink, trout that could not live in the sea.
And themselves, one dry day, stepping where they had
never been, not born here, but bound now to this
salt-free spring which could take their knees and hands
and lips, turning each of them into a body of water
through which the tearless Truro fish could swim.

ELEGY IN CASE THEY WIN

We have come to expect it—
   a last minute fold, a sure
descent after the All Star Game
   into the bottom of their division.
No one blames the writers
   in the HERALD, in the GLOBE,
for predicting the past and keeping
   our hopes level with reality.
Hope springs eternal, it is said
   in some other city. So today,
on the verge of victory, on capturing
   the league championship and more,
we mourn the death of our team's
   losing streak. We remember the losses
we could count on, to bring us through
   the off season, to April's lovely
destiny, on Fenway's opening day.

ROUGH FLIGHT INTO BOSTON

The wind could have brought us down
   into the whites of their eyes, the harbor's
froth, onto the backs of swans and the swan

boats. Carried us against the tide of traffic
   onto the golden bulb of the statehouse,
into that rich hill that blinks like a beacon.

The wind could have swerved us over
   the river like paper hovering a vent,
over the crews of students pulling their shells

through the blue tide of exams, the Charles latex
   rats. The wind could have hit us against Fenway's
green wall, bounced us on the parquet floor

in the Garden in the North End, under the T.
   The wind could have piled us against the teeth
of Kennedy, the one light of Revere and the two

shots of Bird, the hat trick of Orr. Shaken us
   into the ink of Hancock, the speech of Paine,
the drawl of Dorchester, taken us between

the breasts of Gardiner, her courtyard flowers,
   her dusty Titian. The wind could have thrown
us into the bay of lost r's and the r's

added to any idea. Why did Salem hate its
   women? Would we take Harvard's new
drug or pray like Mary Baker Eddy?

Would the wind know to push its own bright
   button, dropping us to the lobby of Logan's
runway, leaving our hearts in our throats up here?

WHILE WE ARE WAITING

No word from Mars yet,
although it's more like
a tick or a tap the scientists
are waiting to hear, just
this side of the millenium.
Even an anarchist in Seattle
stops for a minute to gaze
up to the stars before kicking
out a plate glass window.
We don't know if the lander
is speeding through time and
space, having missed the red
pinhole of its target. Mark
McGuire, Earth's man from Mars,
said you can't take your eye off it
for a split second, if you mean

to hit it a mile. How about a hundred
and fifty-seven million miles
as a mark to hit? I don't know
if anything's speeding toward us,
tonight, looking for a soft landing
here in Middlebury, Vermont,
or if that ticking is a mouse
inside the walls, heaven-sent,
we could say, for us to hear,
while we are waiting for some word
of what the silence sends.

NORTH/SOUTH

for Bob Pack

In the long run for both of us
it will be the willow darkening
in a northern twilight
as the dominant key of winter

reasserts itself. As even now
in late August outside this window
the small birds hesitate among
the branches before they arc

their bodies south for the three
days' flight above the darkening
waters. Angel-winged they turn,
before they lock on their own

essential homings. Or, to see it
from your perspective: flight
to a southernmost extreme. Robert,
for whom if not for you

could I feel this bond, your north
anchoring my still-vexed south?
Even these so-called free-verse
lines arc in a double *pas de deux*

pan-foot, goat-foot rocking back
and forth, playing counter
to that granite bass of yours.
You grin that flinty grin glistening.

MOUNTAIN VIEW WITH FIGURES

As if Cézanne had rendered it: a palimpsest
of planes, a dreamscape realized, an imbrication,
the easel facing the brilliant south exposure.

In the middle foreground a patch of vale, shadowed
by a swirl of crosshatched pines. He counts again
the colors: a tan, a green, a gray, a tan, a tan.

Beyond the graygreen strokes he feels the Absolute
malignly beckon in the bald & treeless peaks.
He stares now as he contemplates his labors,

the hesitations hissing up ahead. It is
what has kept him sleepless night after night:
fear at the edge of the abyss, empty speculations

deep enough for even an Empedocles. He knows
the most he has to paint with is a round
of absinthe sounds & acrobatic stanzas. Those

and a syntax even the boys at the Sorbonne
could nod assent to. He wants the words to paint
his naked canvas, words to ring in the Absolute

at last. He wants to feel the mountain ring.
Fool that he is, he needs to feel that, if he
climbed it now, he would find himself transfigured.

LANDSCAPE WITH DOG

Often up the back steps he came
bearing gifts: frozen squirrels,
sodden links of sausage, garter
snakes, the odd sneaker. The gnarled
marks are still there as witness that,

confined, he took his tensions out
on doors & tables. And life went on,
& mornings, peace & war, good times
& depressions. Pale sticks turned
to trees, boys to larger boys, then men.
Icestorms, wakes, elections came & went.
And always he was there, like air,
a good wife. But then there's this

to think about & think about again:
the last time I saw Sparky he was dying.
His legs trembled & he kept moping
after me. I remember trying to get
the stubborn mower started, June blazing
& grease & six–inch grass & sweat,
& no time then to stop to pet a dog.
And having no time left himself,
Sparky simply lifted off those
cog-wheel scrawny legs of his,
& turned, one of the best things
life ever handed me, and lay down
somewhere in the woods to die.

NEW ENGLAND WINTER

To hell with John Greenleaf Whittier
and his chirpy snowfall odes. Snow.
We've had our share: 18 storms thus far,
ice layered like so much sandstone shale.
A regular archaeologist's dig.
All the television graphics show
this at least: a winter made in hell.
Each day now proud old records fall,

to be replaced by miserable new ones.
What fun it is to sit here counting
off minus 30 mornings, these glittering
kitchen pipes festooned with ice.

On the upside, take the Angelinos after
last month's quake, fear mounting
with the mounting Richter Scale,
the decibels revised upward. Twice.

"Maybe, but I'll still take the quake's
twenty seconds to your hundred-day
glacial siege. *Anytime.*" Thus my
California sister, who *can* be tough.
What hours, days, I have spent
reading the West Coast fault lines from L.A.
on up, all the way to the Aleutian chain.
"At least we're built on firmer stuff,"

I feel myself edging to a crushing
rejoinder, this once vindicated. But by then
she's off the phone, no doubt
outdoors already, tanning on that delicious
cedar-toasted deck of hers which gazes
so serenely out over the Pacific Ocean.
While here am I, iced-over & snowed under,
blinking out this frozen glass. At this.

A BREAK IN THE WEATHER

Done in and travelling west yesterday
down over the WPA bridge connecting
Sunderland and South Deerfield, on my way
to see the dentist (a tedious half-

terrifying way to spend a morning:
the horse needle filled with novocaine,
the droning highspeed drill, the boring
ride alone) half-past nine and warm enough

to nudge a crocus out of its benumbing
winter sleep, grey swales of greysplotched
grey on grey, erratic windswept drizzle,
the swish swash of milk- and oiltrucks slashed

across my trenchslit vision when, all at once,
out there standing on the midspan of the bridge:
a young man wrapped in a forsythia-yellow poncho
and bearded as some scholar of the Talmud.

Before the Mack truck lumbered splashing
into view, I got to see this place for once—
saw it through another with his eyes shut,
arms bent upward at the elbow, hands cupped up

and rain streaming down his face. There,
just there behind him: the world opening south
to the horizon, unfolding like some giant crocus,
as the clouds swirled stippled grey and white

in bold strokes above the southward
crowding river, as once atop Mount Washington
I remember with winds whipping the glacial scars
and once as I suppose it must have been

those years ago, when horned with radiance,
Moses stood talking with his God. Pilgrim,
stranger, whatever you care to call yourself,
you who stood there above the waters

spelling the Connecticut, my thanks for waking me
to such splendid weather before the traffic
crashed back over us again in torrents
and I lost you in the slanting rearview mirror.

GATEKEEPER

It's a relief when it goes:
the thrall of leaves, a demiurge
in the treetops, after the bliss
of waiting gold. Before the dead season,
we recognize the dead. The dog searches,
nose down, trailing something rank
to roll in, to wear as the sign of who he is
under the thumb of Saturn—the god
who ate all his children but the ones of air.
What's left, I wonder
in November, but the shimmering ground, still
lit with leaves, their feast-like colors
underfoot. On the path to the river
I see the shape that lends the land
its rise and fall. Clarity informs me
like the distant-eyed
gaze of the chipmunk left at my door,
the hour it took to die, the quiver in him
driven by a disbelieving heart, his back legs
rowing and rowing, nothing in him so great
as the need to get up, get to the other side.

THE OWL

How far did she fly to find
this pristine town on the edge of winter?
Crows have set up their kingdom—
a yacking flock louder than the traffic
maims the morning air.
Day sends the coven screaming
in pursuit, black rags
haggling from clump to clump

of the decorous elms and oaks.
The dog's mouth hangs. I follow his gaze
through the shudder of limbs
to the still source, the center
of their flapping. The barn owl
commands a branch, the crows scatter
and aim, cutting around her
placid weight, something more of earth

than air. She stares straight ahead
as if focused on something she alone
can hear, their outrage at who she is
no more than a furious snipping,
until in one motion, she heaves upward,
her body transformed by sky.
The crows gloat, their battering
closes her path, and she misses a beat,

stumbling in the air
like a silence disrupted. The crows'
fat riot, their mine, mine, mine,
rules the sky. Call the owl
sadness, the one who watches
from the other side.

INTERMEDIARY

When she came back, my daughter
brought November's moonless nights,
hunters and the frenzied deer,
gunfire over the hill—a world
exposed under the bare trees.
She heard the dogs, and didn't sleep.
And though I couldn't stay awake,
I wouldn't leave her room,
tea at my elbow, my crossed arms
propping my head. I needed to keep watch,
vigilance was all I had—

unlike the hospital, the ones who taught her
to use what she knew, a medicine
in small doses; how to go back
and forth, traversing darkness
as if it were a footpath. It was hell to me,
watching from the other side
of the one-way glass. All I could hear
was the slight buzz of fluorescence,
the stainless walls guarding
her white skin. I couldn't touch
for fear of leaving some mark; my hands
might hold her back from the work
she had to do. They'd hardly let me visit.

I was no guardian. I never knew
what she knew, never followed
through the woods, down to the river,
the abandoned tracks running beside it,
useless steel in the litter and weeds.
Her new habits frightened me, her mouth
a stranger's, a tic in the pause
before she let herself speak, the healed
crosswork of cuts under the chiseled
blue stone that hung at her neck.
She'd found another mother, a faith
that pulled her from her bed,
guided her across the swollen river
posted with warnings, where the trucks
loaded up the carcasses.
Cigarettes flickered, an oil fire
blazed in a drum, sign of the season,
and she waited there,
a knitted skull cap pulled low;
waited for the men, asking
How will you bless this?
How far can you carry this meat?

SEAWEED WEATHER

For three days we've been enveloped by rain
thrashing the house, flattening the sand dunes.
Battleship waves are crashing in tiers of porcelain,
dove-white foam that turns dirty-brown as it's strewn
over mountains of seaweed. Should we regret
the scant shore left? The current could swallow us whole.
The wind's exhale in the volleyball net
strains its fastenings and shakes the two poles.
Somewhere, halyards telegraph a high-pitched—
paean or jeremiad? As ligustrum knocks
the pane, an owl, rarely heard in these parts,
repeats there is nothing but trouble docked
here, alongside a wish, hunkering down
in seaweed weather, to ride the dark squall out.

ALBUM

Bring back the long summer after fourth grade
with stinging-cold waves that crashed on the Cape,
the tall, white dunes we scrambled across, the wild
blackberries we picked, a pair of tame pintoes
fed clutches of grass over the farmer's gate,
Little House on the Prairie devoured in bed—

back the rust-red, overturned rowboat my father
perched upon wearing Bermuda shorts and a grin
beside my gleaming, willow-thin mother,
tow-headed brother, and me who smiled with ease
at the shutter's click, the future assuredly bright,
back the damp days and salt-air night on the skin
when fog drifted down like a cotton coverlet
and at dawn was gently gathered up again.

IN MOUNTAIN AIR

As people were long mistaken about the motion of the sun,
so they are even yet mistaken about that which is to come.
The future stands firm, but we move in infinite space.
— RILKE

The field slopes to a river
camouflaged by summer birch and jack pine,

darkly braided except where light breaks
touching the smooth rocks, the bracken.

Through mown hay, a man and woman walk,
carrying part of their lives.

The only sounds are the trees stirring
and grasshoppers reaching new ground.

Their footsteps do not fracture
any of the mountain's certain stillness;

the grass springs up covering their path
as the roadside inn fades behind.

This time, when they reach the river,
she does not turn away, though she intended

merely to say, *how lovely the evening,*
how level the light traversing the field.

My life is fixed as a table setting,
the distance from the house to the barn.

DRIVING NORTH IN WINTER

All the way to Mercer these
rooms left out
in the dark—

lamplight and two chairs
the old couple sit
reading in,

a table where a family
comes together
for dinner—

the rest of the houses, one
with the night. How
blessed they are,

the man hanging his ordinary
coat in the small world
of a kitchen,

the woman turning to her cupboard,
both of them held
from the cold

and the vastness by nothing
but trusting
inattention

and one beam of light,
like us passing by
in the darkness,

you napping, me wide awake
and grateful for this
moment

we've also been given, apart
in our way of being
together, living

in the light.

THE UNSPOKEN

Was there a funeral for him, the husband
who took his own life? If so,
it was unannounced, as he himself
had been, following the river bank
with his rifle and coming out
of the woods behind the town office
where she worked alone, that determined
she would never leave him, though she tried
one last time, crouching under the desk.
Filling the church to pay their last respects
to her, none of them thought to ask
about him, yet as they rose to speak,
he was the one they couldn't quite
find the words for. "A tragedy,"
said the neighbor who went into the barn
to put out the flames, not guessing
the husband had set fire to the house, too,
and was dead inside it. "This brave woman,"
said her confidante, meaning the alien
anger the wife could never escape.
"Her loving spirit," said the sister,
who understood that when the wife laughed
and fussed over him in the general store
or at the town meeting, it was not love but fear.

WHAT THEY ARE

Not the four wheels,
but clusters of four

and six wheels spinning
into steel hollows
far below the cab. Not a cab,
but high, dark windows
under a crown of lights
and a vast grille displaying
its name: Papa Bear,
Snow Man, Silver Eagle.
Not a truck, but a bird
lifting up over the hill
outside Rumford with a long,
straight tail of logs,
or in the north woods
a ship drifting down, its tarp
swelling in the rain and wind.
Not a ship, but a starship
landing on the night streets
of Presque Isle, lights in the doors
and all along the roof.
Not a roof, but a bed
for lime from Thomaston,
or a cement mixer slowly
turning, or a sleek vessel
for milk from Kennebec
Valley farms. Not one, not once,
but many, day after day,
passing above us
like great Buddhas
with headlights in their knees
and small hands resting
at their windshields
on roads all over Maine.

SHOVELS

Who could have guessed he would choose
to spend so much of his time bent over
a shovel, one wrist so weak he wore

an ace bandage on it, his asthmatic lungs
forcing him to stop for breath again
and again. "Never mind," he would say to us,
his three young stepsons, when we stopped,
too, "get back to work."
                              Every weekend
for a whole winter, we hauled cinders
from the paper mill to level the driveway.
That next spring he had us digging holes
for the barn's corner posts, angry that we kept
fighting with one another in our anger
about the endlessness of banging our shovels
into the nearly frozen ground. Why did he
drive us that way? Why was he so hard
on himself, always the last one to come
in the house out of the dark?
                              One summer
we dug until we found ourselves inside
a waist-high trench he said would bring water
up from the river to the plants of his nursery.
"You'll never get anywhere," he told us,
"until you learn the meaning of work."

Above ground in the moonlight, as I return
through this poem, the tall grass has no idea
where we laid that pipe. The sprinkler system
for the nursery, dead for years, has forgotten why.
All the truckloads of fill we brought to prevent
the bank's erosion are on their way down
into the river. In the back of the old barn,
its aluminum siding curled from the weather,
the shovels we once used stand upside-down
against the wall in the window's light like flowers,
making a kind of memorial to the work
we did then, some with blunted points, some
scalloped at the center, where after all those years
of shoveling, they shoveled themselves away.

STARLING

I lift the lid, reach down the stove's cold throat,
    touch soot and speckles

stunned by this cylindrical pitch of night,
    by solid nothing.

Raise the unblinking body, a feathered
    oil spill stuck

to a delicate spool of bone. Shorebird,
    snowbird—soaked-up

infused rag of rainbow now. My skin,
    unnerved, burns

starlight, star bright, first star I see tonight,
    and, hovering,

my grandmother is humming in my ear. But where
    did you go, my darling?
Starbird, oilbird, ragged bird of yearning.

FLOWERING TREE

There's not enough light yet to know
what color they are, but all the flowers

are moving. Now the blossoms
dissolve, now they are birds,

their pale gray fluttering on hundreds of branches.
Of all the possible forms—indefinite

millions—these birds
swaying in drunken clusters on crabbed, fermented fruit;

their talk, small and intimate.
I try to step inside

but the whole thing wobbles and
takes off, a canopy

of feather, leaf, and petal in the shape of
a tree. All the words

fly out of the room. Whatever was there,
I might have stayed in this world

forever without seeing them,
or feeling their giddy

arrival in my skin, or tasting
in my mouth the color in the tree.

LILIES

I'm not in the mood right now
for physics and its misty
distances, where first our senses
and then our concepts collapse
on themselves, exhausted, and
the parts start falling freely
and forever inward, any more
than I want to think about
the man who took his hand
off with a power saw and sent
the videotape to the FBI
to protest the bureau's pursuit
of his brother for packing tins full of
explosives and flooring nails and setting
them off in public places.

It doesn't matter which direction
you think—in or out,
large or small—infinity
keeps drifting past. No,
I'd rather look at this vase full
of daylilies and Stargazers,
their long elegant throats,
the way they press their faces right up
close to the world, their stories of heaven's
brimming over to make
the Milky Way, the extra splash
to earth, the redoubled consonant
and vowel of the milk's
long fall into such translucent
flesh, cells left partly
open for the gods. But what about
the third brother,
the one who wants
to imagine an ordinary life?

LISTENING THROUGH SNOW

Underneath,
mice and shrews are moving,

the dog can hear them down there,
out of sight and reach.

Your hunch may be right
after all, we take

so many things for granted. Thermostats,
refrigerator trucks. When children

wait in a clump at the curb,
their faces expectant and resigned,

the yellow bus will come.
The dog's body grows still

and fills again with listening,
visibly, the way a glass fills.

What do you suppose
it's like, that crawlspace

under the snow? Low ceiling,
a whole landscape laid out

in a blue-gray glow, the hue
of aerial photographs in wartime,

cities in grids, pockmarked
and pitted, messages painted on walls:

*Everyone from this house
has been rescued.*

*Dear Mrs. Simon, where are you?
We have looked everywhere.*

THE GROVE AT NEMI*

Then and *after* were no use to me, nor the desire
to make permanent the impermanent.
The significance everything takes on after rain
was no use to me. I'd come back and it
was not there, not the least shining.
Sometimes there came
one with whom talking went on: *How does foam?*
How does play of light? I would watch the lips
plumping up, the mouth
flapping
its wings, eddying the syllables.
It was like looking down
from a great height.
When below clouded, there was under
with its violaceous twilights, there was down
with its thunders and echoes. On one of my walks
there was a bridge. Was it
ambition I lacked? In its raiments
of cobalt and brown, the river
was naked.
Most sublime achievements, I began.
Bedizenments, I said. *Investiture.*
Toward evening, birdcalls
became stranger, wilder.
What does strange? What does wild? Beyond
the lumber camp, a sound
of flowing,
exultant, indefatigable.
Was it sublimity
I craved? Huge trees were piled up, some
stripped of their bark, and the roots
of a tree dangled
from a machine. In the sky, creamy
utterances. Foamings.

Toward evening, a hugeness.
Some of it moving toward me,
but most of it retreating. Into itself.
Into greennesses untitled.
The flowing splintering, breaking
open, strewing itself.
The surface of the flowing uneven, bumpy.
In places, the hugeness
blurring, opaquing the vacillations, the quandaries
where it hesitated over leaves, over
branches bent into the asides, the digressions.
Toward evening, — *What does evening?*
What does open?
What does does?

*The wild grove where the Golden Bough was said to grow in a sanctuary sacred to Diana. Located in the Alban Hills, Nemi and its lake, which the ancients called "Diana's Mirror," still exist. But the locale described in this poem is actually northern Vermont, and the river is the Lamoille. Where the Lamoille River approaches the town of Johnson, there is a lumber camp.

PUSSY WILLOW (AN APOLOGY)

Why delay? Today I stopped
to rub the fur, like the tender
ear of a cat, stopped

to stroke the lush gray
plush (and oh, the pink!) as if
the cat had rasped

itself to frenzy, to an
ecstasy of itch
all raw.

this steak tartar, this
chafe of meat, and
because of this

I was late (the willows in
their bins outside
the florist almost as tall as I)

and once again, have traded
friendship for
dillydally.

I had to take off
my gloves, and I would have
taken off my skin

(for why should I put
a barrier between
myself and anything?)

to pluck, to blow back
each separate tuft
of foam (in down, sink down)

because I cannot keep my hands
off the world and the world
out of my breath. What

does the world want (anyway)
of me with its pussy willows, with
its tears and angers

its greeds and splendors, its
petitions of
skyscrapers and waterfalls?

And what do I want with
its famous and forgotten? And is
this the purpose of my life,

to figure this out? Or is it
to touch and be touched? And if
I love the world more than

any one person, or if I love
one person more
than the world, what

does this say of me?
And what do I say to friends
when they keep me waiting,

Oh dally, friend, delight
so that I may rub
it from your body

its furs and gewgaws, its
horrors and sweetnesses, so you may
deliver it to me, you

the messenger, the unwinged
the prosaic in all
its scratch and bliss?

THE KISS

He said I want to kiss you in a way
no one has ever kissed you before, a kiss
so special you will never forget and no one will ever

we had moved into a room away
from the others where coats were piled
on a bed, and in the almost dark the kiss began
to assume baroque proportions, expanding
and contracting like a headache   pushing winglike

from my feet. In adolescent fantasies I used to
think of myself in the third
person so that when I kissed for the first
time in a film of my own making a voice
kept saying Now he is kissing her, now she is
unbuttoning her blouse, now his hand

the voice just ahead of the picture or the sex
lagging always behind as in a badly
dubbed film   the voice

trying clumsily to undress them, hiding
behind a screen or hovering above the bed dovelike
a Holy Spirit of invention presiding over each
nipple, enticing erect the body's
erectile tissue, inflaming their eyes

to see in the dark hiddenness
of wordless doing, to watch, to keep watching
to the edge of, the verging precipice beyond which
language, thought's emissary huffing
and puffing, or beyond which language's undercover
agent and spy, thought.   Now thinking back to
that time, I am always just behind myself
like a shadow, I am muteness
about to blossom   into mystic vision   or with some word

stick a pin into, fasten like a butterfly
on black velvet, though it seems forever since I
kissed the back of my hand, pretending
my hand was my mouth, my mouth
the man's, in order to know what a kiss was, teeth
gently pulling at the skin on top
near the knuckles, the way a cat lifts
its kitten by the nape of the neck, dragging it
to a dark place under a house, or

licking the inside of my hand up the heart
line, down the life line   I don't

remember who left the room first, though
when someone told me he was
a famous director, I watched more intently
as he held out a canapé
to his wife.
                    Sometimes in the years
that followed I thought of him, his ornate

description of the kiss, which with time became
more ornate, his tongue glossing

the whorls and bric-a-brac, the Adirondack
antlers on the grotesque banquettes, the kiss
coiling round itself like a snail

a small Gorgonesque affair with all its
engines thrumming, that description the most
memorable thing about him whose face, if I ever
really looked at it, I have forgotten,
whose mouth, whose teeth, whose tongue
did not open anything in me
but directly

presented themselves as one takes a pear or apple
into one's hand and walks down the street
not thinking about the apple
or pear, but simply eating.

BEING WITHOUT POWER

(The Great Ice Storm of 1998)

The first truth known
to Adam's family
must have been alone
for a while. The world's first fact
came like an unwelcome guest,
cheerful, absolutely without tact,
who casually appropriates your home
when you want rest.
That truth: a sense of having less,
the knowledge of having lost
and being deprived, to operate in darkness.
To eat cold food you're tired by
oddly, still makes misery,
as it does to lose one glove. Why?
In part it's maybe that we need to possess
signs of what we'll never be.

Not that we doubt we'll see
restored to us in time
each convenient luxury,
but there's an ancient ledger
where silken bookmarks peek out
and hint at lost original treasure.
Lost by a gaffe we could never see
but hear told so much we listen with pleasure
as to stories of when we were babies, so perfect,
and we start to believe that we remember,
that someone loved us, we observed,
so much that again
we took it as truth,
as new fact then,
that it could last. We deserved
it. Then came the proof.

IN A NORTHERN SPRING

The chorus line of crabapple trees
so bare just now
in the taut season of skin and bone
stand with upturned limbs
like Cretan priestesses on the point
of beginning the ritual.
They pray the clouds to come, as drops darken
their splitting bark.
Only the form, an attitude toward sky
reminds us of some absent
rite of fruit, or leaves or fourteen days
drenched in blossoms' incense.
First inwardly we clothe them with memory's detailed faith
in an old promise,
then watch them stand to be healed by sacred rain
that cannot stop kissing.

CONUNDRUM, MAINE

to my father

Why when I drive through
a snowstorm, at that
swallowing moment when the
center of the possible shrinks
and recedes to the point of
light that grinds out the snow,
why at that sample
of dying by flying head first
into the now of snow,
why do I see only your eyes?
Or why does the work of raking
up from the dark cave
those dry wild leaves landed
on the floor of my lazy archives
make me dream your sibylline biceps?

Why do I through the wind
hear your voice
saying the names of the trees?
Why do I?

ROCKY SHORE

Even if it feels unusually futile
to wait here for what we know
will not sort itself out,
some great suspense holds us.

The only superpowers ever,
earth and sea,
in ancient stalemate
yield near equilibrium
again today as one thrusts
toward the other that eats
away edges from a retreating cliff.

Surface heaves and threatens as nothing
disrupts the stasis of salt
between storms and daily battering,
where nothing stops because nothing started.

Holdfasts as good as roots
fix to rocks the fronds of sea's weeds,
the floating hair of all those hostages to quiet.
Acorn barnacles fight tides to hold
to one bony purchase, while dog whelks
worry them and bore toward
flesh in the rush to change
what can only work at balance.

Rapprochement at best but
no détente will slacken
this elemental fight
to make a desert
and call it beach.

ON THE STRAND AT PLUM ISLAND

from a photograph by Bob Orsillo

What if the earth knows longing and regret,
And no one's heard a whisper of it yet?
Why is the earth without an intimate?

These cursive lines, in which the ebbing tide
Would hint at little secrets to confide,
Denote a frilled coquette and not a bride.

Sometime the waters' cool and tapered hands
Withdraw, and bare the belly of the sands;
Who then admires most least understands:

A cold reserve is in the artist's eye;
And science only questions how and why.
The hovering gulls take sustenance and fly,

And wheel again and swoop and never tire,
And that approach is closer to desire,
But—satisfied with little—lacks its fire.

Of all the lambent forms that pirouette
In space, might one not be a Juliet?
Why is the earth without an intimate?

True, the moon returns at time's insistence,
But, then as now, the moon will keep her distance
And offer but reluctant coexistence.

The busy-body dawn makes one forget
The dream of her recumbent silhouette.
Why is the earth without an intimate?

WIDE BRUSH

"Vanity of vanities, says the Preacher; all is vanity."
— ECCL. 12:8

Late afternoon, in the slant winter light,
Where men are painting the white buildings white,
The shadows of their ladders climb the walls
To meet the covering darkness as it falls.

SALT MARSH

Do the grasses of the marsh ever sleep?
Confused in new light, beginning to stir,
they have the look of just awakening
from dreams slow to lift, slow to drift away.
The sun comes early to visit, and stays
the day. They are good friends, all gathered here.
They have time. They have so much time to spend.
First one trill, then a distant chorus calls
notice to the seconds and half-seconds . . .
The listener hears and does not hear. Time
is and is not, both at once, everywhere.
See how the wide circle of the sky fades
where it meets the low hills. The long grasses
shimmer from here to there. The sound of birds
trickles from an unseen spring. Sudden
multitudes of wings fan and thrum the air.
The feathers of each wing are made of light.
Green-to-gold, wine red, straw with trembling seeds,
all combed amiss, the grasses of the marsh
jostle and yearn after the coursing wind.
Startled, beneath the tufted hummocks runs
the cocoa-brown mole in his labyrinth.

MARCH WINDS

A wintry storm's blown over us while we slept.
The world's no worse for it,
Though a storm-window cracked a bit
When it fell down hard in the middle of the night.
All we value most we've kept.
The tree of life is still upright.
And now behind the racing clouds some patches
Of the vaguest blue
To which any human hope attaches
Show through.

For lack of sleep the trees are deaf to reason—
These other trees I mean.
They half-create the bleary scene,
Gesticulate against the leafless sky.
Who could trust this nameless season
Dressed in the rags of one gone by?
But underground another current passes
Quickly, serpentine.
Some gladder rumors whispered in the grasses
Hint of green.

OLD COUPLE AT HOWARD JOHNSON'S SODA FOUNTAIN IN MANCHESTER, NEW HAMPSHIRE

He steers her in like a baby carriage.
Places each jointed part
in the seat. She stays
where she's put,

all but her mouth, which neither
of them can control. Unhinged,
it stands open.
Anyone can look in.

He's attentive, smiles at her cheekbone.
She stares straight ahead,
a soldier obeying some unsaid,
inflexible orders.

He has bacon and eggs, she has a malt.
Wonderful! she picks it up,
drinks. He leans to wipe
her naughty mouth.

Try to see the girl he married
walking beside the Merrimack
wearing a picture hat, noticing. Before
the river froze.

Is this love, the kind it takes years
to make, or the Christian kind?
Or a case of not cutting off your leg
because it's asleep?

Amor vincit omnia.
Drink up and get home.

AT BOSTON PUBLIC LIBRARY

In the Humanities Room
the windows are barred
but it's warm and dry
and the books don't edge away.

Never mind if cheap wine
is a flower that
breathes from lapels
and broken zippers are smiles.

So what if this woman
who finds a lost son
stuck in the copier
sings him a lullaby

if the captain's raincoat
is three inches short everywhere
and he fell into sludge
and forgot to wash after

if the one in the coonskin cap
has misplaced his socks
the one in the wheelchair
snores at the fiction.

The librarian's busy.
Overhead the fluorescents
say *hmmm* while defeat
compiles its anthologies.

ON THE CLIFF WALK AT NEWPORT,
RHODE ISLAND, THINKING
OF PERCY BYSSHE SHELLEY

The house of stone turns its back on town
to govern an Atlantic even sky can't stop.
Big as a museum, it keeps us off the lawn
with chain-link fences camouflaged by rosehips.
Presiding from this height it says *Look on
my works, ye Mighty, and despair!* I do,
counting forty windows, six French doors,
a dozen chimneys. Gone, the men who
ushered progress here, those individuals:
who breakfasted on the green, debating wars
their women wouldn't understand. Farewell.
The waves still fling their ermine to the land,
refine the rocks colliding in their pull—
a loud applause that steadily makes sand.

APPLE-PICKING

The trees are falling
down the hillside
down into the valley
of the town of Stowe
falling with the
weight of apples

the branches sag
with red balls
it is Christmas
and Isaac Newton
walks among us
as we walk amazed
among the apples

apples tempting
apples throwing themselves
at our feet, apples diving
into our mouths, apples

apples, today is
the birthday of the apple
and we are glad to be
here you and I
and our 2 native golden
delicious, their cheeks bulging,
chins dripping, mouths pressing
sweet juice from this earth
this planet Apple.

AFTER FIRE IN RIPTON, VERMONT

There it isn't

the white house at the edge
of Robert Frost Memorial Bridge.

Instead three black mounds, proof
the house has buried itself.

One wall's become a billboard
advertising without words,

a red wagon on what was lawn
sings *ashes, ashes, we all fall down*

and on the clothesline, blues and yellows
tangle like a vow.

Aldous Huxley said when his house burned down
he felt clean.

Today purification clogs the air,
I can smell it from my car.

This could happen to us, this cure—
"Some say the world" etcetera—

a frayed cord, a languid cigarette,
or wind the rider no one intercepts

and next morning, desire's zero:
the presence not here.

LIVING WITHOUT

Out is never content to stay there.
It's not enough that we're in it,
but out must be in us.
Our house in the woods, the wood of our house;
the ants, bees, wasps, flies and mice in our house,
the cold in our house,
the birds we feed at our window.
The lines of separation blur and dissolve until
I cannot tell where the woods stop
and I begin, the difference between
the feeding birds and my own hungry hands.
We are in the territory of the wind,
and it lets us know, constantly
shifting, clearing its throat,
muttering to itself—and under cover of night—
pushing at, and sometimes shoving
the house an inch closer to somewhere
or an inch further away,
until one warm night in March
when we open the bedroom door
and watch the curtain arch into the room,
slim, and grey in the dark,
the wind fiercely, exultantly, in at last,
and never more other than now.
Perhaps it's the suddenness of the change
I cannot accept.
All month the snow has melted reluctantly,
almost invisibly, its white-knuckled hands
guarding the secrets it has kept all winter—
and now, this fierce warm wind in the night.
I close the door and pull the blankets up to my chin—
but the wind is in.

RED GLOVE

The red glove in the road
   this morning is in the tree
this afternoon, angled

so it seems to be waving
   hello, something cheerful,
or something cautionary

like a cop waving me on
   past disaster. I straddled
the glove with my car

without thought
   or connection, my life
a life apart from yours, mine

as yet unmarked by loss.
   Some mishap, little
or large, led to the

glove being left
   in the road, someone's
care hung it

in the tree. That's what
   we do here, something
I've done myself—

placing a glove on a storefront
   window ledge, mailbox,
parking meter, a strictly local

lost and found. Perhaps
   you'll return and find
the bright glove

in the bare tree, a signal like
    the return of red-winged blackbirds;
the beech shedding last year's

translucent leaves. I was the one
    supposed to die driving, nobody
was supposed to die now.

The effect of your
    absence, something
that can't be measured

or qualified by any paradigm
    I know, like the effect
of the glove in the tree,

like subatomic entities, it
    can be defined as a particle,
and also as a wave.

If physics are right, you've
    only been changed, not lost, if
we're whole in every

part, and all part of the whole—
    you're everywhere. Between
the glove, bird-bright and

frail in the road this morning,
    and the sign in the tree
tonight, I've had news

of your death.
    Will there be a sign
to tell me if

you finally find ease
    and comfort, if your glove
finds its mate?
                    for Lynda Hull

JANUARY THAW

Mostly, the snow had melted—
   what remained held, then gave, held
and gave, beneath our feet.

White pines creaked with light wind.
   You stood in the clearing—lips pursed, making that
pish-pish-pish sound that you have always claimed

will bring chickadees right to you, but
   today you also
held your hand outstretched and

full of seeds. Chickadees materialized
   before us, circling,
daring near and nearer perches.

One passed, inches from your hand—
   considering. The hand remained steady,
the seeds unmoved. The chickadee

passed—and passed again—
   landed on your hand and stayed a moment, but
fled without seed—the good you had to offer being less

than the danger you might pose.
   The bird fled to a further branch
to recover balance, then passed,

passed again, and finally,
   making the decision so much more quickly
than I had—landed on your hand

and picked a seed; cracked the hard shell
   and took the meat—
mature and sweet.

BALED HAY

Wheels of baled hay bask in October sun:
Gold circles strewn across the sloping field.
They seem arranged as if each one
Has found its place; together they appeal
To some glimpsed order in my mind
Preceding my chance pausing here —
A randomness that also seems designed.
Gold circles strewn across the sloping field
Evoke a silence deep as my deep fear
Of emptiness; I feel the scene requires
A listener who can respond with words, yet who
Prolongs the silence that I still desire,
Relieved as clacking crows come flashing through,
Whose blackness shows chance radiance of fire.
Yet stillness in the field remains for everyone:
Wheels of baled hay bask in October sun.

WILD TURKEYS IN PARADISE

Just down the slope from my own deck,
two apple trees I planted years ago,
now fully grown, stretch out their arms
as if they are enjoying the late warmth
of the November sun.
They bore so many apples that
I let them ripen unplucked on the branch
and fall, according to the rhythm of the year.
Such bounty piled up on the ground
the grazing deer could not
consume them as they rotted and turned brown,
and I could smell their pungency
when wind blew from the east

until the first snow came and covered them.
Last Sunday, strutting stupid from the woods—as if
                    no hunters stalked Vermont—
            six turkeys gathered by the trees,
        bobbing their jowly heads beneath the snow
to slurp the apple nectar, so fermented that
                    just twenty minutes later
            they were reeling, and their eyes
blazed with amazing knowledge that transported them,
        within their bodies, into paradise.
                    Despite their drunkenness,
        despite the ice that kept them shifting one foot
                    to the frozen next,
            they kept their balance in a dance
    of bumping lightly up against each other,
                    circling, brushing wings, and then—
            as if their inner music paused—
they'd dip their heads back underneath the snow
                    and lift them up so high
            their necks stretched out to twice their length
to let the trickling juice prolong their ecstasy.
            And thus unfolds a moral tale:
                To be plain stupid is
        to be divinely blessed, and lacking that
transcendent gift, an animal advanced as I
                requires a holiday
            to cultivate stupidity, to choose
                    one Sunday morning to know
        nothing of ongoing hunger but
            my body trembling in the sun,
        drunk on itself, so that right here on earth,
            right now, I tasted paradise—
as, so to speak, in talking turkey, I now do.
            My pilgrim mind has taken flight
                and then returned to join
    my body stomping in the snow; and so
                I raise a toast to say:
I give thanks in behalf of six dazed, drunken birds
                that grace the icy view
            beneath my apple trees today!

LATE SUMMER PURPLE

Wild aster, bee balm, phlox, chrysanthemum
Proclaim pure purple in the pallid dawn,
Asserting there's more blossoming to come,
More purple in the prickling thistle thorn,
More purple in the valley's swirling haze;
Even the robin's shadow on the lawn,
Even your welcome of the dwindling days,
Proclaim pure purple in the pallid dawn.
Pure purple is the color of your need
To have your mood made manifest, your final flair
Before October's culminating leaves exceed
In parting opulence the purple air
That radiates about your head
As if dispensing rapture everywhere
You move to make a purple hymn to hum:
Wild aster, bee balm, phlox, chrysanthemum.

MOUNTAIN ASH WITHOUT CEDAR WAXWINGS

The likely last nostalgic warmth of autumn
     has gone by, the amber leaves
have fallen from the mountain ash, and still
        luminescent berries
    hold their positions on the chill,
stiff branches, clustered together like orange stars,
    because no cedar waxwing's come
       to stuff its horny mouth
       in preparation for
   its migratory journey south.
Listen! for I'm no longer sure I know
    what words can reach the words in you,
      though words have been my life,
no cedar waxwing's visited my tree
     four bleak falls in a row,

after a quarter of a century
　　　　according to my watch,
　　because their southern habitat
has been deforested at the dumbfounding rate
　　　　of eighty-two square miles a day.
And watching their not dwelling here a while,
　　　　watching the silent way
　　the orange berries seem to cry out
for the yellow blur of flurried wings
　　　　that gives the gaudy gold
　　of autumn its autumnal burnishing,
　　　　summons to memory
　　the losses I could not have known
life on this planet would inflict on me.
　　　　I knew I'd have to face my aging
　　　　and my death, but not
the death of forests, not of oceans, not the air;
　　　　I knew I'd lose my parents,
　　　　lose unsuspecting friends,
　　but not the bond that lets us share
　　consoling voices from the past,
not faith in our true mother tongue that seemed,
　　　　hardly a rhyme ago,
　　generative as April mist,
evocative as February snow.
　　　　But now, dishonored and demeaned,
language itself, like ravaged earth, betrays
　　　　its own betrayers who
　　betray the laughter Chaucer knew,
betray Shakespearean remorse, whose mind,
　　　　beyond all anger and all tears,
　　　　as breeding as the sun,
could empathize with everyone.
　　　　These are not losses of my own,
　　　　losses that I can bear,
　　　　my temporary life,
but loss of what I once thought permanent—
　　the woods, the oceans, and the air,
　　　　loss of the binding words
that mean the meanings their intenders meant.

Is it too late for me to say,
    for better or for worse,
I feel as empty as my mountain ash
    without the cedar waxwings here,
I feel the loss, wide as our universe,
    of everything that I hold dear?

ODE TO A LOVESICK MOOSE

*Experts at first thought the relationship between the lovesick moose [Bullwinkle] and a
Hereford cow [Jessica] was only a flirtation, but now the nuzzling has gone on for nearly
two months. Baffled animal behaviorists say it may be true love—at least on the moose's
part. "He just has these mixed-up feelings, something between passion and
companionship," said Charles Willey, Vermont's moose expert. . . . Tony Bubenik, a
retired moose researcher, said that he simply thinks the lovesick moose is a little bit
immature.*

    —THE BURLINGTON FREE PRESS, DECEMBER 16, 1986

Sing heav'nly moose, you baffler of behaviorists,
    of love, abiding love, beyond
        flirtation and the tease
of nuzzling Jessica amid the Hereford herd
    among the sullen cedar trees

muffled with snow, beside an ice-edged stream
    in star-crossed Shrewsbury, misty
        at ominous, red dawn.
Still unrequited in Vermont, you are prepared
    to wait until all snows are gone

at this appointed place, unlikely landscape
    of romance; your muddy state
        between companionship
and passion, no!, is not mixed-up or immature—
    rather, I see your spirit grip

its fate in this harsh world, implausibly
    incarnate in your patient bulk
        so seemingly astray.
O, expert disbelievers, look at Bullwinkle,
    see how he guards her daily hay

and rests his muzzle on her back, then gazes
 at the darkened sky, his love
  transcending what the genes
of other species-bonded moose ever could know
 even among the freshest greens

of the eternal fields of flowing spring.
 Divine mutation, holy moose,
inspire new love in me, beyond my horny kind,
  for the dazed cow of Earth
 now grazing sunlit in my mind.

SWIMMING IN LATE SEPTEMBER

We listen:
the hush of apples falling through a dark,
the crackling of pines.
A slow wind circles the pond
like an ancient bird with leathery wings.

I float, my belly to the moon,
lifting my toes through cold, black water.
You brush against me, fanning your hair,
so close we are touching head to foot.

Frog-eyes sparkle in the ferns
as if they wonder
who would be swimming in late September.
Already the crickets have lost their wings;
the woods are brittle yellow.

But we go on swimming, swimming.
It is part of our love.
We give off rings of chilly waves
from one still center. Tonight
there is nothing but skin between us:
the rest is water.

SKATER IN BLUE

The lid broke, and suddenly the child
in all her innocence was underneath
the ice in zero water, growing wild
with numbness and with fear. The child fell
so gently through the ice that none could tell
at first that she was gone. They skated on

without the backward looks that might have saved
her when she slipped, feet first, beneath the glaze.
She saw the sun distorted by the haze
of river ice, a splay of light, a lost
imperfect kingdom. Fallen out of sight,
she found a blue and simple, solid night.
It never came to her that no one knew
how far from them she'd fallen or how blue
her world had grown so quickly, at such cost.

THE LAKE HOUSE IN AUTUMN

There's silence in the house at summer's wake.
The last leaves fall in one night's wind,
the mice are eaten, and the cats begin
a rumbling sleep. There's nothing much at stake.
It's not quite cold enough to stoke
the furnace, and the neighbors never seem to mind
if leaves are raked. I'm staring through a blind
at less and less beside a cooling lake.

I keep forgetting that this absence, too,
must be imagined. What is still unknown
is still beyond me, as with you.
The mind is darker, deeper than a windblown
lake that tries to mirror every hue
of feeling as the season takes me down.

A KILLING FROST

Beside the pond in late November,
I'm alone again
as apples drop in chilly woods
and crows pull tendons like new rubber
from a roadkill mass.

Ice begins to knit along the ground,
a bandage on the summer's wounds.
I touch the plait
of straw and leafmold, lingering to smell
the sweet cold crust.

An early moon is lost
in sheer reflection,
wandering, aloof and thinly clad,
its eye a squint of expectation.

I know that way,
this looking for a place to land
where nothing gives,
these boundaries of frost and bone.

THE RUINED HOUSE

Deep in the woods, beyond the shuffle
of our works and days, we found a path
between an alley of Norwegian pines.
The children ran on spongy needles,
disappearing in the purple shade;
their shouts were lost among the bird-yip:
tremolo of wood-doves, long diphthong
of redwing blackbirds, crass old crows
all harping on the same old note again.
Your hand in mine, we seemed to drift upon
a fuzzy cumulus of half-voiced thoughts:
the tongue's quick shuttle through the loom of mind
in search of texture, text to sing,
recitativo of a thousand glimpses
caught, composed. All along the way
the eye sought gleanings, images to tell,
to cast one's thoughts on, fix the swell
of meaning in the cross-haired sights
of metaphor, a trope to end all troping:
words and things in pure performance.

Now the hilly path went straightaway ahead,
unfolding with the ease of morning vision.
As they would, the children found it first:
the ruined house on what was once
a breezy hillock in an open field.
The coarse foundation might have been
a dry stone wall like other walls
now winding over hills, down dingly dells,
to parse the complex sentence of our past,
delineating fields no longer found,
obscured by popple, tamarack and vetch.
The stone foundation of the house in ruins
wasn't stern or morally suggestive.
It had just withstood what it could stand—
the falling stars, the tumbledown of snow,
sharp dislocations of the frosty ground,
the weight of timber soaking in the rain.

We stepped inside behind the children,
who were walking beams like tightrope wires
across a corridor that once led somewhere
warm, familial, and full of light.
The cellarhole was still a hutch of night:
one saw it through the intermittent floorboards
and the two-by-fours exposed like vertebrae
that once held everything in place
but powdered now and sagged toward the middle
as the woodmites fed and moisture softened
grainy fibers, as the mulch of days
began in earnest. There was still a roof
aloft amid the trees, a fragile shade
with patches that were open into sky.
The children clambered up a tilting stairwell
to the second floor; we followed suit,
though not so fearlessly and free
of old conceptions—hurtful images
that hold one back, making one wish
for something less or something more.

*

The little bedrooms that we found upstairs
were still intact, with built-in beds,
coarse empty shelves still half considering
the weight of objects from their rumored past.
If one stood still and listened close
the voices of the children could be heard,
their laughter in the leaves, the sass and chatter.
Anyway, that's what I told the children,
who believed and listened and could hear.
It's not so hard to frame the past
upon the present, to connect the dots
all still in place, to resurrect and ride
ancestral voices: there is one great tongue.
We find ourselves alive in that old mouth,
through which all meaning flows to sea.
We pour and pour the water of our lives,
a glittery cascade, its brightness falling
into pools where it must darken once again,
must soak in soil, collect and gather
in a place to tap for future soundings.

Later, in the shade behind the house,
we lingered in the garden's dense enclosure.
Petalfall of spring was planted there,
the hard ground turned, the weeds uprooted.
Beans and flowers were assigned to rows.
While he would ditch the upper pasture,
she was left alone sometimes in summer
and would sit there safely in the chestnut shade
to read the Brownings, he and she,
as children napped or slaughtered dragons
with their makeshift swords. That's how the idyll
runs, of course. The typhus and the cold
that cracked the windowpanes in mid–November
and the bitter words: these, too, were true.

We left on hushing feet like thieves
with something in our pockets, awed and fragile.
It was only time that turned those pages,
leaving dust in sunlight on the stairs,
disfiguring the walls that once would keep
a family aloft through hazy fall
and hardy winter into sopping spring.
It was only time that would not stop,
that bore us homeward on the needle path
toward the end of what was ours
a while that summer in the leafy woods.

WHEN I DREAM OF ETERNITY

It's like this: late September
and all along the stone shore—Camden, Rockport,
Booth Bay, Bar Harbor—the boats are drifting home
with the almost human scent of rotting fish and sweat.
The tourists are gone—the young girls, arms naked
and burning in the sun—the boys who chased them
in old cars, hot and sulfurous. The vendors have closed
up shop. And the town is left to the abandoned
shipyard, its rails empty and running into darkness,
to piled lobster traps that dry and rot, to the second
mortgage, the grocer bill, to the bone-white spire
of the Lutheran church reflected in baywater,
engine-sleek and shining with the last flame
of evening. There is the hungry cry of gullsong,
a hollow report of wood on wood and the quiet chatter
of the last ones on the docks, tying off their boats,
exhausted, shoulders swaying drunk with work—
Unbreakable, timeless as the sea, they will make
this last as long as they can. Forever if they have to.

MUD SEASON

The thing about remembering is that you don't forget.
—TIM O'BRIEN

Vermont. Ripton. It comes when the ground gives way
from six tight months of frost—red clay, soil, dung, softened
with the moan of aspens and the oak relaxing into April
as a hard man's fist unclenches from a ten pound maul.
At evening. With darkness. And you can't keep it out.
Creeping into bootleather, canvas, jeans, your skin. Following
you home, across the fields, into your house, floorboards,
bed sheets, years of dreams. Where people have lost things—
whole fields of boots pulled down and smothered, chain-saws

wheel-barrows, left out, sunk, taking root. Once
behind the old barn, down the sloping pasture where
the east field meets the spring I watched a team of men
struggling to pull a horse from the earth. His forelegs lost
to the kneecaps, his chest down and forward as if
he were bending to drink, or was caught in descent, leaping
a fence—a moment's grace where time doesn't seem
to move or matter—but there was no grace in this. He fought
or tried to fight, pulling against his own weight which only
made each leg sink deeper. I remember the whites of his teeth
and eyes bared clear, whiter with fear and muck. I remember
the sound of screaming, throaty, desperate—the ropes tightening
around his waist, his legs, and the men pulling, digging, cursing
the mud, the horse, the rain, themselves and sinking still. And I
remember thinking they were all part of the same beast, brown
and heaving from the earth as if a great oak were trying to uproot
itself from the banks and walk. It was dark and raining. I was
cold and colder for being young and younger for being hopeful.

Don't ask me how this story ends. You know. And even now
the telling feels like a sinking in. Miles away, years gone and still
when I hear the loud crack of branches in a March storm I feel it
in my chest, a breaking in the breath hitting full force, a gunshot
hovering somewhere in the tree-limbs. And I know that I
won't sleep or worse, will—having given in to the night,
to exhaustion like some great heaving animal, its legs broken,
closing his eyes at last, sinking into the earth.

CAGE CRY—SHARON, MASSACHUSETTS

"Good fences make good neighbors"
—ROBERT FROST

Too many, they are too many; and for months
they have been coming—out of the woods out
of the soft green hills, driven south and east into
the suburbs by hunger, starving for predators.
And the town wakes to a cage-cry of chain
on bone, sharp, brittle with sunlight, the bark
and howl of dogs gone mad with heat, years

of thrown stones, the taunts of children and now
this—something wild, bleeding and caught

in the wrong world. At the gate, an officer shifts
nervously, as the deer dodges quick and smooth
leaping and falling again in bright, terrified arpeggios,
notes escaping the scale like Mozart or Bach but
rushed made strange and desperate. And the dogs
don't know what to do exactly—take short runs
at the hooves, back off, snap growl whimper. Caught
somewhere in an old instinct, suppressed, trained out

but calling still. He slips a hand to a gun
he has never used before in a town too small for guns
—where the best that can be done is clean up
what is already gone wrong beyond all anticipation—
dredge the body from the lake, pull the child
from the car, seal off the scene, hold the head
of the suicide while his father screams and life spills
through your fingers to the floor. The deer makes

another run at the fence, leaps, fails—breast-fur
reddening; the dogs cry, metal wails, and the man makes
a soft gurgling sound in his throat that could be laughter
or the exact sound of fear, or love when there is nothing
to be done but stare on helpless—as it wheels, gallops,
sprints suicidally past. They are all frightened beyond
all logic, having passed contact, impact, deeply into pure
sense: smell, taste, tar—salt—iron. One leap and it rises

rising impossibly and comes down, slow—a windbent
poplar stretching toward earth; the sense of green
wood straining and the surety of breaking; then,
changing, a flute-note held beyond the capacity
of lungs, a movement that escapes all composition,
escaping the maker itself, and touching down in a space
beyond fences, beyond help and the need for help—
a moment that lingers and somehow doesn't come
and is gone all at once—a deer passing into the woods
at last, into the silent starving of a small New England town.

WOODSTOCK, VERMONT

My brother's new farm
sits near a hill's foot
and just a mile up the road
from the ex-French teacher's place
who now speaks Cattle.
After we tour the house
and talk logs, we hike up
the hill's back, spot tracks
that look dog, but we know
are deer, then find an old
stone wall that fences in
a herd of pine.

From the porch Tom points
to mountains that don't reach
our chins. If we had the rock
it took, we too would let skiers
slide down our sides for kicks,
turn our heads peak
but make sure to keep our names.
Looking across the road that ends
in sheep, I notice scarves
made of smoke keeping homes,
neither of us can see, warm.

After coffee we chop wood,
joke our dead uncle back
as a brook near the barn that never stops babbling,
then stack the rest of the day
against the house.

Later we drive into Woodstock
for dinner at Bently's and a walk
through town. Shop windows

are already red for the holidays:
a crystal of hymns are sung
by a choir, flowers flare with all
the paint they have from a bouquet
of dishes and geese fly north on wine.
Other windows are simply red
from the cold.

Homes are steeped in history
and snow. We near a wooden bridge
whose roof is shaped like hands
praying for a warm winter.
Tom and I stroll through, knowing
we are just two more prayers
that can never be answered.
On the street a shattered block of ice
reflects chunks of night. We walk
around it and back to the car
making sure not to step on
frozen pieces of moon.

A SPRUCE IN VERMONT

Trees grow in sky
until I spot a mountain
and know it's not clouds
they root. In the distance
another mountain is my
height—even with its snow
cap we stand eye to peak.

A stream runs down
a deer's throat until
my boots crack twig
and spook it back
into mountains that slope
for no ski.

I stop my climb to rest
letting my eyes fill up with view.
I watch the river, my map
claimed was pink and flowed
on for inches, curve
with the hope I lost
the first time a mirror
made me stop and whisper, fool.

And the pride I thought
hid in a man's chest
near lung or heart is just above
my head in the quiet
an eagle slides over,
cleaning away clouds until
it shines with sky.

I've decided where ever
that river begins I want to end
like this wind that dies
then comes back again
in another gust.

As soon as the last mourner
prays me warm and on my way
my feet and hands root
grave, seeds twig upward
from my ears until one breaks
ground as spruce with a trunk
of the strength skin could never give.

What little money I had
means nothing compared
to the rich soil I horde with shade.
Then I bud April out of March early
so spring can get going
and flare July so green
I make the next faithless man stop
and figure God one more time.

VILLANELLE IN APRIL

One night the beavers breached the dam and fled
Leaving a rutted crater in their wake.
Suddenly her water floods the bed.

Come out and hear the woodcocks court! he said.
How curious the ruckus that they make.
That night the beavers breached the dam and fled.

Two adolescent hawks wheeled overhead.
Later she sees their figure-eights in the dark
As suddenly her water floods the bed.

We've had more rain than we anticipated.
The weather hovered over tea and cake
The night the beavers breached the dam and fled.

It's somewhere between a rock and a loaf of bread:
She laughed. *But how much longer will it bake?*
Afterwards her water floods the bed.

He sang: *The antiseptic scent of melted
Snow, The season opens like an egg!*
The night the infant breached the dam and slid
From her. The beavers slapped their tails and fled.

SEPTEMBER AT THE HOME

Her hands still farm the sheets.
When years outweigh the body, I perch
by her bed and whisper, *Speak to me.*
Chrome catches the diamond ring that

hangs from her finger as a good dress
would from the rack of her spine.
By God (she swears) *You'd better
believe*. We fill the larder, pare

core and quarter hours, scare up jars
of relishes and jams, mince, quince.
Lestoil douses cinnamon. We talk down
dim stairs where a new screw-in electric

bulb shaped like a summer squash sheds
light on all she's squared away. We slip
tomatoes from their skins easier than
children, shuck and strip cobs' milk-

sweet, sticky silk. We tackle pickles:
bread & butters in pints, dills in brine
kept crisp with grape leaves, cool in the
crock held down by a plate and rock.

You have no idea how much we had!
she cries. Harvest holds
us in place. Our laps heap,
famous with all we have named.

*

No patch to tend, no man
to escort them through a reel
or cornfield: my hands hoe
their deeds. We put words by.

THE GARDEN IN WINTER

doesn't need us, wants to be still,
cold, unforthcoming,
not hurried into life

by the glamorous deceits
of a sudden thaw. Yet we can't
help being happy, smelling

the earth again, our jackets
unbuttoned, the dog romping
among the sticks of the field.

But the garden knows
that whatever appears now
will wither, that we're wrong

to want what cannot survive—
we who pretend to know better,
swayed so easily by desire.

EMILY DICKINSON'S HOUSE

"It is true," Emily Dickinson wrote
one day, looking out
of her window, "that the unknown
is the largest need of intellect,
although for this one one thinks
to thank God." Almost all my life
I've lived not far away,
and I've never been to her house.
I don't know if her desk
is near a window,

or what she'd have seen
through the wavy glass: trees, sky,
another house, the familiar
facts of the world
which she knew must be resisted.
Or learned so well
their strangeness is restored
each time we look: maple and elm,
clouds or sun, then rain,
the neighbor's house (a man inside
reading a book), and then
the unseen moor, and the narrow wind
that sweeps across it.

HUNTERS

This last cold winter killed the flame bush
at the edge of our meadow, although I'm sure
those hungry deer helped it along.
They should have eaten less.
Next year if the snow's as deep
they'll have nothing. But they're all
so tame and stupid they stand around that field
in the middle of hunting season, as if they trusted
the signs that say Keep Out. A farmer
in Vermont used to paint cow on the sides
of his cows and they still got shot.
And I've heard that serious hunters
dress in camouflage, figuring that even a red vest
could be some drunkard's idea of a deer.
Somebody's out there in the cold with a gun
thinking, Man and Nature, Mortal Combat,
and then a flick of white—
how could he tell it was laundry?
Or his friend unwrapping a sandwich?
It's the price we pay for woods nearby.
I'm not complaining. So many others
have it much worse all the time. Step out

on the street at the wrong moment
and it's over. You were in their line of fire,
or you looked like somebody who'd just
burned them on a drug deal.
Or maybe they were driving by and since
you were nobody one of them said,
"Let's blow that guy away." It was bad luck,
though if they'd known you, and if
they'd needed one, they would have found a reason.

THE HORSE WANTED SUGAR

Sascha shivered where the mare'd licked her hand.
December, when things should be ending,
but Sascha picked up twigs and shriveled berries,
even tufts of frozen grass and invited them

to her palm, the horses. Did I wish she were mine?
Did I look into the wind that brushed our faces numb?
Did she show me the way to make them chew,
stroking their noses and singing nonsense tunes

in their ears? I could mention the stinging tears
and the whining that followed in a meadow
whose sole shelter was an old stone fence
and a mangled maple bent over a pond.

In a flash she wanted to be home where she belonged.
So I raised her on my shoulders and we galloped for a mile,
neighing and crying, till her father met us at the door.
I blew into her hand and hung her snowsuit in the closet.

"The horse wanted sugar," Sascha said. "But we fed him a leaf."

I JOIN THE SPARROWS

Let me join the sparrows
in the snow. As one of them,
I'd stir the kingdom up
and to their busy fluttering
add a chirp. If I could
make a sound to satisfy
the heavens, like wind
through paper, a harp

of wings, if I could join
the kingdom of the startled
constantly, I'd lose the snow-
capped mountain view,
the death I earned, laboring.
God, speak to me
through sparrows, insist
we're not waste and water.
The sunlight fading
late December holds no lesson
for the living. Perched
on earthly wings, above
the bog where sparrows mate
and make their home,
I'd sing awhile, a high, faint trill.

I LIKE WAKING UP

I like waking up by the lake
frozen over, the frosty meadow
where a white horse still huffs and chafes
by the fence post and a few fog clouds
cling to the tree line of the Sugar Loaf range.
I like the lake a block of ice. A few years ago
I would have said *paralyzed,*
but I didn't live where Linda wakes now,
her children lightly breathing a wall away.
And until a logging truck trudges by
on our dirt road—its chains rattling—
we have a moment together. I'd like to say
the world began this way: on the cusp
of winter: Five A.M.,
no gunshots, no sickly deer
limping asymmetrically
into the clearing. Before still water
turned to gnats and mosquitoes,
the algaed pond that murky, turquoise green
we make of things.

SPRING THAW IN SOUTH HADLEY

Old snows locked under glass
by last night's ice storm left
curatorial Winter, in
whose hands alone we'd hope
to find the keys,
jangling them in the trees—

not merely in these pine
needles by the fistful
gloved in crystal, but,
from their boughs, the self-
invented digits of
icicles addressed

(in a manner reminiscent
of the insubstantial
finger of a sundial)
less to a point in space
than effectively to Time,
the frozen moment.

By noon, the ice as thin
as an eggshell veined to show
life seeping yellow,
one's boots sink in
with a snap; the sap
underrunning everything

may be nothing but water, yet
there's a sacramental
joy in how, converting
to its liquid state,
it's anything but gentle.
A crash from Abbey Chapel—

who cut the string
that sent the white sheets falling?
Nothing but the long
scissors of the sun
unwraps such thunder. Even
a modest A-frame

in a muffled instant sheds
its wrinkling roofs of snow:
black butterfly below.
As if to make
one more clean break above,
the sky—seconds ago

one continent of cloud—
follows the drift of Spring,
splits and refits like Ming
porcelain. The plate
tectonics alternate:
white and blue, blue and white.

READING ROOM

Williston Memorial Library,
Mount Holyoke College

The chapter ends. And when I look up
from a sunken pose in an easy chair
(half, or more than half, asleep?)
the height and heft of the room come back;
darkly, the pitched ceiling falls
forward like a book.
Even those mock-Tudor stripes
have come to seem like unread lines.
Oh, what I haven't read!

—and how the room, importunate
as a church, leans as if reading *me:*
the three high windows in the shape

of a bishop's cap, and twenty girls
jutting from the walls like gargoyles
or (more kindly) guardian angels
that peer over the shoulder, straight
into the heart. Wooden girls who exist
only above the waist—

whose wings fuse thickly into poles
behind them—they hold against their breasts,
alternately, books or scrolls
turned outward, as if they mean to ask:
Have you done your Rhetoric today?
Your passage of Scripture? Your Natural
Philosophy? In their arch, archaic
silence, one can't help but hear a
mandate from another era,

and all too easy to discount
for sounding quaint. Poor
Emily Dickinson, when she was here,
had to report on the progress of
her soul toward Christ. (She said: *No Hope*.)
Just as well no one demands
to know *that* any more . . . Yet
one attends, as to a lecture,
to this stern-faced architecture—

Duty is Truth, Truth Duty—as one
doesn't to the whitewashed, low
ceilings of our own. Despite
the air these angels have of being
knowing (which mainly comes by virtue
of there being less to know back then),
there's modesty in how they flank
the room like twenty figureheads;
they won't, or can't, reveal who leads

the ship you need to board. Beneath
lamps dangled from the angels' hands—
stars to steer us who knows where—

thousands of periodicals
unfurl their thin, long-winded sails;
back there, in the unlovely stacks,
the books sleep cramped as sailors.
So little time to learn what's worth
our time! No one to climb that stair

and stop there, on the balcony
walled like a pulpit or a king's
outlook in a fairy tale,
to set three tasks, to pledge rewards.
Even the angels, after all,
whose burning lamps invoke a quest
further into the future, drive
us back to assimilate the past
before we lose the words.

No, nobody in the pulpit
but for the built-in, oaken face
of a timepiece that—I check my watch—
still works. As roundly useful as
the four-armed ceiling fans that keep
even the air in circulation,
it plays by turns with hope and doubt;
hard not to read here, in the clock's
crossed hands, the paradox

of Time that is forever running out.

THE UPPER STORY

As Emily Dickinson
would not come down, I'm
sorry, but I've felt the need to climb
the worn steps to her room,
winding up the stair
as if into her inner ear.

Art, as she once said,
is *a House that tries to be haunted,*
and as I stand
on the landing where she curled in shadow
to follow the piano
and soprano voice of Mabel Todd

(her editor years later—
who now graciously accepted
a poem and glass of sherry in place
of having seen her face),
this would become that House.
No trespass can erase

what she once made of it—
that gate she opened, resolute
to escape, and just as quickly shut:
*I think I was held in check by some
invisible agent . . .* And when she wrote
Again—his voice is at the door—

here is the door she meant.
Her room, probably Spartan
even when lived in, now holds but few
fabled artifacts: a snow-white
coverlet; a "sleigh bed," narrow
like a wooden shoe; a snipped

lily of a dress, limp in the closet;
a wilted hatbox; a woven basket
she'd lower, something like Rapunzel,
full of gingerbread.
Or so our guide has said. Yet
devoted to the genuine

as she was—first jasmine of the season,
hummingbird and snake—
I doubt she would have taken umbrage
when learned men in Cambridge
spirited off her writing table
to higher education. A double

(its surface little more
than two feet square, and where
poems commensurately small
were scrawled on backs of envelopes)
sits convincingly beneath the tall
window onto Main Street.

To shut our eyes is Travel,
and that table may as well
be anywhere as here.
She'd have held close whatever house
she was born in, as a squirrel
palms its acorn; but with a need

not wholly fed by fear.
At twenty-four, moving back
to her birthplace, she'd lived the thought
transposed: To travel, shut the eyes.
I supposed we were going to make a "transit,"
as heavenly bodies did . . .

She was truly half-
astonished at those carriages
and cartons—almost as if
she'd lived only in that other life,
unseen, in her upper story.
Touch Shakespeare for me,

she wrote to Mabel in Europe,
thinking her close enough.
Why had anyone expressed the hope
to see Emily, who'd compare in letters
her unmet friends to Peter's
Christ: "whom having not seen, ye love"?

Finding nothing and no time
impalpable, she'd call
attention to the Biblical
"house not made with hands" for all
who'd listen. Wasn't that her home
as much as this was? Fame,

a lower form of Immortality,
in the intervening century
has unpacked her cradle to restore
its place, steps from her deathbed.
There is no first, or last, in Forever . . .
To the West, across the field

from another window, lives the family
at The Evergreens, whom Emily
saw little more than I can: Austin
and dark sister-in-law Sue.
I would have come out of Eden
to open the Door for you . . .

but she hadn't had to.
Drumming down the stair,
my ears fill with the spirals of a fly
a poem let in and won't be shown the way:
as if that buzzing, when she died,
were here still amplified.

AUTUMN PROGRESS: RURAL VERMONT

Here, another season of mellow fruitfulness.
Bees drowsing in fallen apples, maple leaves
leading where they've always led: downward
to stubble fields.

One county over, in the exploding
suburbs, dirtroads are smothered—
the oily scam of macadam—and
pastures bulldozed of their bulls.

Listen. Listen hard. You'll hear it:
the *beep-beep-beep* of something backing up—
backhoe, dumptruck—sweeping up what's past,
then moving forward, closer to our future.

Let's break the law and put a billboard
on the county line. Let some old nature
goddess gaze out on the two-lane and speak
a mouthful to the passing motorists:

New mansions of Jericho,
let your walls tumble down.
New malls of Saint Albans,
let the season's sweet decay

inform the air where shoppers,
clutching purchases, whirl past
on their way to checkout counters.
How little you'll take along:

not your blackamoor lanterns and pink flamingos,
not your Saabs and Volvos parked in tractor ruts.
Measure progress by what trees
give back to the forest floor.

Measure it by pastures mown of their excess.
The blades will lie down easily, revive
without past-lives of grass-crowns
to slough off.

TRUSTING THE LAND'S PURE CURVE

*"There is seldom more than a man
to a harrowed piece."*

— ROBERT FROST

(for Roger Peterson)

I.

    how after walking through choke-cherry blossom
you come to a mossed stone wall. Where there's a gap
in stones you think "gate and cobbled roadway,"
and take it back further into forest.

Losing the road in dusk, you pocket compass
and survey map, go by the land's pure curve—
back between those younger trees where pasture
was carved, stumps plowed under, and one
small-farmer lived after his own way.

Further on, you read another dozen
stories of faded farms until you come
to their Vermont town and rest on the rusted
seat of a model T, smell the rotting
barnboard of a general store, and dream
of the Yankees who walked these hard-packed streets.

    how following the road back, you know
there is no road but the one you've made
on a topographic map, your pencil's
broken dashes across the elevation
lines tracing the mind's bond to the land.

2.

Years later, you climb to the place
where a culvert diverts a rushing stream
and learn the calculus by which men
abandon the uncontrollable seasons
of wind and rain. Bodies still vanish

in flashfloods, boulders click like marbles
over sleeping villages. One equation
will build a dam in a river of whitewater
and cast a safe shadow over the towns.

Now you imagine rounding a mountain
turn, to come upon, at dusk, industrious
towns—your way lit wholly with water.

All day these visions glint behind your eyes.
Immersed in the hum of machines, you wander
far from your body and hardly notice
the light dimming to autumn, the leaves
flickering and going out, the trail cold.

3.

The snowshoe rabbits you stalked and caught
huddle in their hutch, perhaps breed safely,
and all their brethren survive. Perhaps
remember the small hungers in winter air,
the thorn in the fur where the hare shivers

in its thicket. Today you regret
the scars have faded where blackberry bushes
once scratched your face. There's little trace of the wild
blood on your lips. Dead leaves have fallen

over the old roads: stone gaps open wide
inside you. Would you walk back now into your life,
trusting the land's pure curve for direction?

4.

Or would your well-trained eyes peruse the lines
of survey maps, conclude the fallen stones
were nothing but the natural fault lines
of the aging world, and turn, and return
home the well-marked way you first had come?

Or would you, as I want you, read those gaps
as stories seeking your return, to take back
further into forest where the voice is
not your own but now the property

of one who lived after his own way,
sleeping easily beside the tumbled
general store where pine and birch thrust
tangled limbs out through the roof and windows.

FROM HAYDEN'S SHACK, I CAN SEE TO THE END OF VERMONT

*I shall have given willingly my eyes
their long holiday.*
—JOHN MILTON

Hunkered here, mid-winter,
Clay Hill hollow,
Johnson, Vermont, along
a cold stretch of roiling
water, it gets dark early.
The darker it gets,
the further I see.
Mind's eye adjusts
its aperture, just as
this old dairy state's
adjusting—just fine,
thanks!—packing up
its milk and maple buckets,
parceling farms, plunking down

silver in the shape
of ski chalets, new bridges
and ridgeroads to get there.

They're moving higher up.
Ayup. This state's adjusting
fine to darker doings,
coating itself in silver.
Make no mistake,
it's getting darker.
No real surprise God's
proverb—*And lo! Your hoards*
of silver shall turn to tears—
comes flooding home.
Mid-winter, this much rain
makes silver of Vermont.
Maples buckle under
ice-coats. Regal
and ruined. Not
a bucket of sap
come spring.

Highwater mark's set
for erasure. Mind
shapes matter,
and the matter here's
a new (bank)roll of images
washing over the old, images
developed in the mind's
darkest rooms, under-
exposed, over-developed.
Hung on a nail, the picture
shows landscape awash in cash.
Don't stand on my word.
Stand behind the lens and look
for yourself. Is that a silver
maple or silver
girder rising
across the river?

One county over,
in the exploding
suburbs, one mayor
is Marxist, another Progressive.
Here, for now, we vote
Cowshit Farmer. Happiest
when old Hippies and Yankees
shovel shit together,
know cowshit from bullshit
imported from elsewhere.
But even here, it's
darkening. Rising
real estate. High-
balls at five.
We close our eyes
to the tale of two cities
nearby, Queen and Capital.

"People's Republic
of Burlington," old Marxist
stronghold, now just a stage
on its way to high
capitalism. Church
Street commodified.
Out on the loop roads
of Montpelier, what does "strip
development" strip? Grass
from pastures, cows
from barns, moss
from stone. Strips
the locals of control,
strips "the local" from our minds:
local color washed, rinsed, blanched.
In the mind's eye, silver
replaces it: silver girders

rising across a lake in Milton
(namesake of paradise lost). An empire—
plastics, this time—pledges its suspension-
bridge across clear water.

The tax-base wobbles and swallows
its last helping of hemlock. It's getting dark.
Vermont sports thirty new girders, silver
"reinforced structures" replacing
the wooden ones. Is that the silver
side of a brook trout
nailed to a wooden plaque?
Is that the silver
sky of an ice-storm moving in?
Ice storms are so New Jersey,
so Connecticut. It's getting dark.
Down here in this hollow,
we're already saying grace.

"PUBLIC SERVICE IS RICH ENOUGH"

—that's what my mother used to say,
switching off the bathroom lights behind me.
"Public Service is rich enough," she'd nag,
when I'd leave the downstairs light on, in the hall.

Afternoons, I'd sit at the dining room table
and do my homework in the dark.
When I couldn't see another word,
I'd turn the chandelier dimmer on low,
then dial the lights bright as noon,
dimming them down to dusk, midnight,
and brightening the night to dawn again,
like God speeding through the first six days,
in a hurry to get some rest.

After my mother's funeral, my father and I
lit a tall, seven-day yahrzeit candle
and put it on the stove, on a plate,
so it wouldn't catch their apartment on fire,
its flame nervous in the breeze I made
walking by, disturbing the progress
of my mother's soul on its way to heaven.

After my father died,
packing cartons, locking up the place for good,
I was surprised how dark it was, it always was.

"Public Service is rich enough,"
I mutter, trailing after my husband and my daughter,
griping at them as I douse the lights.
Sometimes, when we're out for the day
and come back after dark
and I've forgotten to turn the porch light on,
from the bottom of the hill our farmhouse

looks like a sooty shell,
and for a moment I think that it's burned down.

But if I've left a few lights on,
the house looks like it's on fire,
flames blazing from every window.
When we pull into the driveway,
and I peer through the screens at the empty rooms —
the open magazines on the coffee table,
unwashed plates in the sink, my breakfast
coffee cup rimmed with kiss-marks —
I wonder whether we're really ghosts
occupying these brief parentheses.

My husband and daughter shuffle behind me
among the mud-room's scatter
of dirty boots and shoes.
I fumble for the key, open the door,
and burst in upon the kitchen's glare.
And as my family rushes past me,
tearing through the kitchen, the living room,
and slamming up the stairs —
it's strange, how, for a moment —
those rooms seem suddenly darker,
empty of them.

FAIRBANKS MUSEUM AND PLANETARIUM

We climb the stone staircase
of the redstone Victorian building,
my father, my aunt, my husband carrying our baby,
escaping from the mid–July heat.
My mother is missing, dead one year.

Downstairs the museum, upstairs the planetarium;
we've waited over an hour
for the next star show to start,
rejected the brochures and guided tour,

killing time, instead, with the souvenir shop's
boxed binoculars and plastic bugs,
rocks and minerals, and packages
of self-sticking glow-in-the-dark stars.

We loiter past the Information Desk
where they've set up a card table with an exhibit
of local flora, each wildflower
stuck in its own glass jar
propping up a smudged typewritten label:
Queen Anne's lace, cow vetch, wilting black-eyed Susans
sprinkling pollen on the tabletop
like pinches of curry powder.

The high barrel-vault ceiling made of oak,
the oak woodwork and oak balconies
shiny as the beautiful cherry and glass cabinets
the janitor just finished polishing,
but all the exhibits inside the cases
are falling apart, from the loons' moth-eaten
chests molting like torn pillows,
to the dusty hummingbirds' ruby bibs.

We interrupt a custodian vacuuming
a stuffed polar bear with a Dust Buster.
The bear's down on the floor with us, on all fours,
pinning a seal under his mauling paw.
Shuttling the baby between us,
we shuffle past a grizzly
rearing up on his pedestal;
his shin-fur scuffed and shiny
where visitors' fingers have touched.
He's in a permanent rage, his bared teeth
stained yellow-brown, as if from nicotine.

The Information Lady hands us over
to the Tour Guide.
And though it is only ourselves, and a grumpy
French-Canadian family with three wired kids
detoured from the Cabot Creamery,

she ushers us up the wooden staircase where we meet
the people from the twelve o'clock show
staggering down.

French doors open and close on the planetarium
barely bigger than a living room,
rows of wooden benches
orbiting the central console
where our bearded, pony-tailed Star Guide stands
and welcomes each one of us
with a damp handshake and a "Hi."

My family sits together in one row,
obedient children on a class trip.
We're present, all eyes and ears.
The sun sets, the darkness intensifies.
Our eyes adjust, our heads tilt back.
Suddenly the starless sky, pitch-black,
dark as the inside of a closet,
makes me feel like crying.
Not a splinter of light squeezes out
from under the french doors' crack.
My father and aunt immediately doze off.
They're tired, tired of missing
his wife, her sister. Now there's nothing
but a big black hole to hold us all together,
the gravitational pull of grief.

'Tim' tells us his name.
With no higher-up to direct him,
he's got his chance to play God.
He pivots at his podium, clears his throat,
and casts his flashlight-baton
across his orchestra of incipient stars,
no music yet, just warming up;
only his voice and a thin beam of light
about to point out areas of interest.
My husband hands me our daughter
and I open my blouse to nurse her.

Tim tells us how he used to chart the heavens
from his bedroom window in Ohio when he was a boy,
then he rehashes The Star Wars Trilogy—
that's what first hooked him on astronomy.
He tells us about his courtship of Annie,
the home-birth of his baby . . .
Every once in a while he remembers
to mention a star.

My father snores softly. Nights and days
are swirling all around us, moons rise and set,
seasons turn, constellations twinkle
on the cracked ceiling above our heads.
Over the planetarium's slate roof
floats our familiar sky,
two Dippers, Big and Little,
and Jupiter, Mars, and the same old moon,
big and yellow as a wheel of cheddar,
preparing to rise from behind our hill.

An hour later,
like the paired fish in Pisces
swimming in the sky, the baby and I
are still at sea, too exhausted
to crawl along the bleachers and escape outside.
The sun pops up, pure Keystone Kops.
My aunt startles awake, gropes for her purse.
My father snores louder.
Fading, the Milky Way shakes over his bald spot—
covered, one year ago, by a yarmulke
as he stood in the cemetery under the trees, in the heat—
under the big dome of heaven
where my mother now lives.

SPRING PEEPERS

Listen, as the cries of spring peepers
like ghostly minnows
swim this way, now that, through
the naked woods,
moonfish seeking their home.

The moon's pale laquearia
flashes upon the water,
the peeping is more insistent,
a whistling tide.
The deep croak of the elders underpins it—

the lime green, the light brown,
the dark green bull with his red earrings
hidden in the murk.
This amphibious symphony
shakes the roots of trees and the nervous buds,

lifts them toward the hologram of stars.
Shrill notes rinse the hollow rocks,
cleanse the hidden waters
running where streams
suck them to the deep ocean.

The frog hibernates in the heart,
come spring, awakens,
leaps and leaps,
sending his laser cries into the blood.
We sleep with short galvanic twitches,

dream of falling,
wake to moonlight burning along the floor,
spilling over the windowsill,
and follow barefoot into the grasses,
our pajama legs soaking up the dew,

down to the edge of the lawn
where the rain makes the ground unsteady,
the thirsty ear drinking in
these arias, duets, choruses,
these nightlong operas, oratorios

of swamp and woods,
these litanies of ascending summer,
from the intimate, singing ventricles of the heart.

LOOKING FOR MT. MONADNOCK

We see the sign "Monadnock State Park"
as it flashes by, after a mile or two

decide to go back. "We can't pass by Monadnock
without seeing it," I say, turning around.

We head down the side road—"Monadnock Realty,"
"Monadnock Pottery," "Monadnock Designs,"

but no Monadnock. Then the signs fall away—
nothing but trees and the darkening afternoon.

We don't speak, pass a clearing, and you say,
"I think I saw it, or part of it—a bald rock?"

Miles and miles more. Finally, I pull over
and we consult a map. "Monadnock's right here."

"Or just back a bit there." "But we should see it—we're
practically on top of it." And driving back

we look—trees, a flash of clearing, purple rock—
but we are, it seems, too close to see it:

It is here. We are on it. It is under us.

WALDEN ONCE MORE

The New England landscape is like a radish salad.
—LENAYE HUDOCK

for L.L. & C.

Comestible, comprehensible.
   heaped up in digestible portions.
Thoreau had eaten far in Concord
   and still this knoll
with its floor of puce-colored leaves
   under May's green mist
feeds the visitor. These trees
   map out silence like pins
a faintly invisible gold
   breathable, drinkable
as we bite into sharp cheddar, brown
   bread, and drink grape juice
at Walden, my daughter's
   illegal cat under my coat.

Some kind of universe turns here.
   Each new leaf is a star, a wafer,
a harvest the golden grasshopper
   above the Boston Statehouse,
the plague of tourists
   (of which we are four),
cannot devour: the pilgrims
   from the Ganges,
the agitated throttles of bikers,
   the hoarse voices that
rattle with aluminum cans,
   the lovers treasure-hunting in the bushes.

Thirty years ago there was little water,
   sixty years ago E. B. White despaired of the litter,
in Thoreau's day the trees were small,
   the train visible as it hooted and smoked to the west,
the ice cutters muffled in heavy coats, busy.

But silence has survived:
    the water is back,
the litter gone,
    the train invisible.
This intergalactic space between trees has survived
    all the calibrated limitations—
this silence of the wren
    whose brilliant plumage no one has yet seen,
this voice that comes up with light about it
    in perpetual astonishment from the blue-green waters
that fill the oval of the bay.

Here among the dim gray maples
    and the white paper birch
the cat scatters old leaves like cut-off wings.
    We finish the grape juice, the dark loaf.
We have not yet seen the cairn
    nor the model of the hut near the parking lot
where the Concord dump used to be,
    but, moving back through this gray
afternoon, breathing last year's leaves,
    we glance at each other—
the four of us—
    our hunger satisfied.

AFTERBIRTH

In calendar pictures, the cow
leans over her calf, a dry miniature
of herself, as if the cow-stork
dropped it clean into her daisied field.
But when I saw the afterbirth, bright red,
hanging from her square backside
I stopped the car and watched her lick
a shapeless package in the grass.
Soon it stood, hind end first, forelegs
knuckled under until need unfolded them,
then he was up, searching her warm belly
to find the milk. I told the farmer

your cow had a calf just now
in the field, wanting him to clean her up,
take it away. Of course he'd seen it
many times, this vivid scarf she'd spun
out of her body's jeweled insides, flag
that made the rest recede, farm, the trees,
the sky, all bleach into a monochrome.
Not apple red or lipstick, or the bloody
evening clouds, but red as deep and elegant
as silk. This parachute her calf had ridden down.

ELMWOOD CEMETERY

Seven A.M. in the cemetery
it's me and squirrels
taking long basting stitches
across the green lawns.
Men pull up in a blue truck.
Coffee steams as they unload mowers,

weed whackers, lift out pruning
shears, tall red cans of gas.
His skin the color of pine cones,
sweeping black mustache,
he mounts the riding mower
like a caliph his sedan. Another,
a boy, working his way through
summer, swings his blade. Music
presses through soft foam pads
as he centers a jar of gladiolas,
lifts a fountain of hydrangea
to trim around the stone.
This could be a field
of unplugged appliances, crows
hopping from cold stove
to cold stove. Granite roses, poppies,
thistles that hint at Scottish
blood, have replaced the willow's
ancient weeping. A few thin
stones, blackened by the rain, lean
on themselves like broken crackers,
warning so faint I have to kneel
to make them out:
"Be assured that death
will close the eye that is reading,
still the heart
that throbs at the reflection."
Emily at five, Anna, ninety-one,
John Hall asleep beneath
crossed swords. What makes this
a holy life? Wet and dark,
their shirts stick to their backs,
their brows run salt.
I'm hot too, walking in circles.
When I pass we speak,
and squirrels, like mad quilters,
stitch between the stones.

COLD

1.

When I open the door
cold stands in the kitchen
like a man in an overcoat
my mother remembers from
the Depression, empty-handed,
needing a meal.

I put the diseased plant
on the porch, a gloxinia,
bloom after bloom, purple
throated all summer. Now
its fierce, arching leaves,
spotted with scale, will relax
into tongues of pale flannel.

You get drowsy freezing
to death. Blood pulls back
to the heart and what's left
in the limbs turns to ice.
Arctic explorers, bedding down
in a snow field, change
almost painlessly to stone.

2.

Another white day. Ten below.
Without coat or gloves
I go out into the calcified
morning to haul trash to the curb.
Cold blocks my nose and mouth.
Frost glints from yards.

As I reach to lower the garage door
my sweater hikes, leaves a chink.
Cold brands my side.
Winter. Small fire. Tin box
of the body. In the seconds

exposed flesh burns
I feel how quickly, how easily
I could be calmed.

WILD CEDARS

I had seen the truck around town,
the words TREES FOR SALE
scrawled like a threat
on its wooden sides. But the work
would cost more if it was called
LANDSCAPING, so when I saw him parked,
drinking beer, eating donuts, I walked over.
How many trees? How tall? he asked,
his face, brown and prickly.

The next day early,
as if his chainsaw were light
as a dinner knife, he took down
four junk trees, and after they were sliced
and stacked, dug thirty holes by hand
and slammed the carroty cedars in.

When he came back a week later,
hugging a fresh tree to replace one
that had rusted, he brought them with him—
his wife and son. She wouldn't leave
the truck, and from there said *He's spoiled,*
of the boy, seven, who had delicate flowers
for ears, and helped his father
carry water to the trees.

When I asked *Did you go with your Dad
to the races,* he answered *No—with
my brothers. My father stays home
and drinks.* Will he grow tall, and fell
and carve and plant more trees? Will he ever
leave my yard—the pale remembered child,
walking past me, carrying water?

FROM THE MAINE NOTEBOOKS

1. Maine

It's not exactly exile
    but it is a place fortunate
    with many trees, lakes, rivers,
    a great coast, beaches, many islands,
if one has the mind making it possible, it is
    some escape from pollution, Big City noise
    and industry. One comes to Moose, one comes to
    Mount Katahdin, one comes to craftsmen,
    artists seeking privacy, studios,
sometimes seeking to imitate Thoreau. One comes to the
Country of the Pointed Firs and more, much more, the world
    good and bad; it's a sort of outpost
    from which I can send letters, poems.
It's a temporary center of the universe if one has the
    art and mind to make it that.

2. Precise pincers, princely refinement

How delicate can you be and
    tough?
ask Emerson, ask the fine pale
    brown-red
of the small crab's shell that I found
    by the beach
of Morse Mountain yesterday, clearest cool
    Maine summer day.
Practical, self-reliant, practicing one's
    walking and grabbing.
Take to what serves you sublimely, to what
    you serve neatly.

3. What got into the sacred and scampering spirit?

The joie de vivre of
    squirrels playing, very young ones

scampering on the grass, then suddenly still,
    suddenly fast leaping,
summer cool morning, alert rolling over each other,
    suddenly running up a tree,
acrobatic geniuses, what got into them?

4. Grayness   Slowness   January

Fog
over snow
certainly a ghost
in New England could learn
how to appear on stage from you,
vague cocoon of blur, ancestors
and tradition and temporary white churches
lingering

5. Who is the blurred thug?

Lug the bear of melancholy
    around,
lugubrious, it will tire you,
    and
soon enough bore the crowd.
    So now
give it, if you can, the Buddhist
    farewell.

6. Spirited look out

Scallop,
your architectural shell is complex,
    intriguing, and
like some churches you have many eyes,
    scientists
find it difficult to count them,
    (two rows of
tiny blue eyes and they grow new ones every year)
    but mystics
like their relatives the scallops find them
    practical for
watching their surroundings. Visual aids for
    salvation.

TWO POEMS

1. Almost falling asleep, surrounded by snow

One learns to hibernate
to be drowsy on gray days,
gray days and more gray days, to be
    very drowsy
surrounded by quietness and snow; again
    it snowed
all night; where was my soul, my memory,
    while I
was asleep? not so far away and certainly in
    my memory
the heavy gray ocean moves. on the Nature of Things
    Lucretius will
have his gray sayings; its somber music from long
    ago drifts into my
mind; if we return to the sea or an authentic
    poem like that
we'll know it's still alive; atoms have moved;
    Adam by now has
had many costumes, cultures, rags, illusions, myths,
    but certain cosmos
made colors and moods have distant alive resemblances
    to something we knew;
grandfathers, have you forgotten me? drowsy I hear
    the relatives of your voices.

2. The snow seemed High Enough but it continues to snow

Heroic mailmen, not armored Crusaders going
    out to kill
but ordinary democrats plodding through the deep
    Maine snow
from house to house, delivering messages too often
    from Advertisers
but some important enough, desired, from cousins,
    former students,
grandchildren; messages stamped indicating we
    remember each other;

don't hibernate without taking the unsayable
    Golden Rule
with you; a sheaf of wheat, a description of a
    birthday party,
someone saying I liked that expression or we had
    another baby.
There are many gold mines that can never be exploited;
    they explain us.

THREE NOTES RELATED TO THE JANUARY SNOW STORM

1. Promethean Persistence

Here it is dark night
and I am in a winter Library somewhere in the cosmos
a few nights after a devastating Ice Storm that has made
    many branches
from many trees all over the state of Maine fall, many
    heavy thuds to
the frozen ground, thousands of limbs as after a vast war
    Scattered all
over the Campus and the forlorn city, here I am in this
    studio shelter
sheltering Plato, Shakespeare, Swedenborg, millions of
    passionate poems,
and I wonder why man continues this, not condemning the act,
    sitting in utter Awe,
why he goes on writing words words words compelled
    as by an
Angel whispering in his ear, why he accumulates and accumulates
    all these volumes
of various sizes and tones as some Knight in the Night, Guardian;
    I lavish
praise at what I stunned call the Beauty of this Attempt.

2. Post Ice Storm Blues

Blues. Collapse.
Exhaustion. Branches and twigs strewn all over
      the place,
like a Civil War Battle Scene but in Ice
      Grayness,
and the battered body as if punched by the
      Ice Man that
Cometh. Telephone Wires and Nervous System
      unstrung.
Cold stew. No ways of heating food. No light.
      No heat. But
now to want you and write some details
      before my hands freeze.

3. The Compelling Mysterious Forces of Age and Winter

Old Tree
poor old Tree
that many a Maine summer shielded me
that many a warm colorful lavish autumn
      unfurled magnificence for me,
now Old Tree Frozen, the worst Ice Storm I ever saw,
      I am stunned and
almost frozen too, one by one, all day yesterday
      heavy fall of
heavy and small frozen branches, watched you, glass
      enshrined,
Old Tree, Totem, Ancestor, Broken, all night
      heard you, heavy
thump thud of branches, a sudden small landslide,
      Old Tree, Grand Father,
now the small slanted street all strewn with broken branches,
      many wires down,
no heat, no electricity, no hot food, grayness,
      gravity and ice,

some limbs cracked, hanging, heavy with picturesque
    glittering ice,
capillaries, the network of the Body's love, its once order,
    exposed,
Poor Naked Ancient Tree, relative to me, little by little
    we break,
Part of Nature, Part of Time, Part of Mystery.

CONNECTICUT IN MARCH

Here where everything is granite—
from the steps that prop the baby
for her first spring photograph
to the stones gossiping in the cemetery
two doors down—even the green
is lined with gray, and from
the blood-red buds just breaking
will come leaves of waxy green
that raise their hands as if in protest,
showing palms of silver.

I have been to California, I have seen
the coastal evergreens, their skirts reversed,
blown seaward; I have watched the ocean
darken and fold, as if drawing out a secret
from the land. I have stood among the succulents,
sun on my back like a shawl of fire,
thinking of wet bark, leaf rot, grass as pale and matted
to the frozen ground as to a brow in fever.

I have tried to love a place
for the helpless goodness of its weather,
the light that spends itself on everything,
confident of being overlooked.
I've traveled north to where
the sun stands watch like a man without trust,
burning all night while his young wife sleeps,
and I have walked Caribbean beaches
where the various blues amalgamate
to a lover's breath, less air than ardor.

But I am married to this late winter bog,
this grayscape, this
aluminum sky that when it rains

reveals the best and worst that can be said
of any marriage: that it endured.

COMPASS

You're a cabin in the woods slung low
with shadow, mattress on the floor,
jeweled boughs and gelid waters,
stove-ash steaming in the drift beyond the door.

In December you're the fragrance of the blizzard,
ice-slag in the parking lot in May
and summer rain that closes in
like tent-flaps. In the fall, you always say

you wish the goddamn leaves would just
come down and take the tourists with them.
Still bare-chested in November, chopping
tree trunks into chair legs, you breathe in

the bitter oaken whiff of snowbound evenings
with a certain smugness. You're the earth
and I'm the moon, one side perpetually chilled
while your great planet's oven churns,

oblivious, its various climates. You couldn't live
here on this island, where the ocean seeps
into the salt marsh, where the beaches shift
indolently south and westward, laced with creeks

the color of molasses—an island without edges,
sprawled and pliant. You're a mountain breaking
from the earth that holds you, igneous and adamant,
tundra-like in aspect, pale hair making

its tenacious way across a sea of scowl. You're
my wind rose, you're my water tower spotted from afar.
You're a walking definition of where North is:
Stay there and I'll find you by your star.

9 _P.M._ STORM

The wind raises the black plastic tarp,
sharp against the culm-soft glow,

the fish-light that is poached from this space, this ligament dark.
Lightning, eager mouth of lightning

above the Bristol Mountain Gap, and the vantage
from the campsite is occasional, punctures

of the curled valley of dusk. August
in the Green Mountains. The lantern

burls into the night, skitters outward,
vibrates with the shadow of a moth's wings—

magnified, swollen, bent.

MORNING

The cows are filing this way again, their breath
tumbling and full against the wooden fences

that chafe with this Vermont winter. Ice rises
from the knotted pine fence, two hands thick,

and there is movement near the milking barn,
as the herd stutters towards the gate, led

by a man in mud-gray boots. Four A.M.—
so early, and such a full, invasive cold, a cold

that sweetens on the bone—and the farmer leans forward
as the forms move by, exhales his own breath

into the steam and reek of the animals,
into the clouds of vapor that rise

through the bulb-lit air.

LIGHTNING SCARS THE SUGAR MAPLE

Incision of heat, cauterized skin of the tree,
a streak of grease that moves from mid-rise, down

to the mint-black dirt. Lightning scars the sugar maple,
it has mouthed suddenly from the mull of rolling thunderheads,

left the trace of its eager work, a rise of danger
through a blackened strip of bark.

A BRIEF DOMESTIC HISTORY

A lonely lonely man has come to our door.
He's looking for our friend, the bright penny
he pocketed years ago, who isn't here.
Widow Douglas when our friend was Huck,
and no one else to spend his worry on,
he settles in to wait. He loves to talk—
relieved to leave his solitude on the porch,
beast on a weak leash—and offers up
polished opinions on politics, neighbors, god,
the meal in the firkin: he's Emersonian,
but fond: with my teenaged son, my Bartleby
(whom he thinks of as Thoreau—i.e.,
smart, judgmental, passionate and spoiled),
he talks sports, its algebra. At last,

announced by a shredded muffler, Bright Penny
arrives, at twenty-five all optimistic
energy, lifting the lid off every pot.
Whitmanic, fresh from the world, full of the world,
he tows along a boy he plucked from the ditch
if only to remind him of himself;
they've come for my son, they lob the usual insults
at him, cuff him—the universal greeting—
and then, displacing the first man's *gravitas,*
the future commandeers the lit kitchen—
noisy, hungry, hairy, mammalian, gendered
but not entirely sexual, even though
there is that carbonation in the air.

Which makes it seem it's the older wounded man
who's Whitman, trying to redirect his need.
Which means the one whose company he seeks,
grown thoughtless from self-reliance, is Emerson,
this time the younger, not afraid of Walt

though distant, proud, as any son might be.
So here's Walt/Waldo, abject at forty-eight,
and Waldo/Walt, magnetic at twenty-five,
something passing between them like a wire.
Or maybe an absence, a missing tether, the wire
loose on the ground. Which makes them, all of them, boys,

these two, and of course the even younger two,
my husband, also, risen from his lab,
redolent of the power the others covet,
thus dismiss—all of them jousting and chafing,
each with his facts, each with his partial story,
none now willing to be seen as ever
odd or sad or lonely, foolish or frightened,
who're gathered at America's long oak table
ready to fix whatever might be broken,
because I make great soup, great apple pie.

THE ART OF DISTANCE, I

Wrinkle coming toward me in the grass—no,
fatter than that, rick-rack, or the scallops a ruffle makes,
down to about the eleventh vertebra. The rest of it: rod
instead of a coil.
           So I'd been wrong the afternoon before
when the dog, curious, eager to play and bored with me
as I harvested the edge of the raspberry thicket,
stalked it from the back stoop to the lip
of the bank and grabbed the tip
in her mouth and tossed it—
sudden vertical shudder
shoulder-level—
               wrong
to read survival in its cursive
spiraling back to the cellar window-well
where it had gathered fieldmice like a cat.
And now, if it meant to be heading for the brook,

it veered off-course, its blunt head raised
like a swimmer's in distress.
                                    The functioning part
gave out just short of me, inside the shade
but not the bush; the damaged part,
two fingers thick, was torqued
pale belly up, sunstruck.
I left it where it was,
took the dog in, and for hours
watched, from the kitchen window, what seemed
a peeled stick, the supple upper body that had dragged it
now pointed away and occluded by the shade,
the uncut grass.
                        My strict father
would have been appalled: not to dispatch
a uselessly suffering thing made me the same, he'd say,
as the man who, seeing a toad,
catatonic Buddha in its niche, wedged
within the vise of a snake's efficient mouth
clamped open for, then closing slowly down and over it,
bludgeoned them both with the flat side of a hoe.

For once I will accept my father's judgment.
But this had been my yard, my snake, old enemy
resident at the back side of the house. For hours,
the pent dog panting and begging, I watched
from the window, as from a tower wall,
until it vanished: reluctant arrow
aimed at where the berries
ripened and fell.

RAVENOUS

High winds flare up and the old house shudders.

The dead should just shut up. Already
they've ruined the new-plowed field:
it looks like a grave. Adjacent pine-woods,

another set of walls: in that dark room
a birch, too young to have a waist,
practices sway and bend, slope and give.
And the bee at vertical rest on the outside pane,
belly facing in, one jointed limb crooked
to its mouth, the mouth at work—
my lost friend, of course, who lifelong
chewed his cuticles to the quick. Likewise
Jane who calls from her closet of walnut and silk
for her widower to stroke her breasts, her feet,
although she has no breasts, she has no feet,
exacting pity in their big white bed.
The dead themselves are pitiless—
they keen and thrash, or they lodge
in your throat like a stone, or they descend
as spring snow, as late light, as light-struck dust
rises and descends—frantic for more, more of this earth,
more of its flesh, more death, oh yes, and a few more
thousand last vast blue cloud-blemished skies.

DOORYARD FLOWER

Because you're sick I want to bring you flowers—
unforced, neither imported nor potted,
flowers from the landscape that you love—
because it is your birthday and you're sick
I want to bring outdoors inside,
the natural and wild, picked by my hand,
but nothing is blooming here but daffodils,
archipelagic in the short green
early grass, erupted
bulbs planted decades before we came,
the edge of where a garden once was kept
extended now in a string of islands I straddle
as in a fairy tale, harvesting,
not taking the single blossom from a clump
but thinning where they're thickest, tall-stemmed
from the mother patch, dwarf to the west, most

fully opened in a blowsy whorl,
one with a pale spider luffing her thread,
one with a slow beetle chewing the lip, a few
with what's almost a lion's face, a lion's mane,
and because there is a shadow on your lungs, your liver,
and elsewhere, hidden,
some of those with delicate green
streaks in the clown's ruff (*corolla*—
actually made from adapted leaves), and more
right this moment starting to unfold, I've gathered
my two fists full, I carry them like a bride,
I am bringing you the only glorious thing
in the yards and fields between my house and yours,
none of the tulips budded yet, the lilac
a sheaf of sticks, the apple trees
withheld, the birch unleaved—
it could still be winter here, were it not
for green dotted with gold, but you won't wait
for dogtoothed violets, trillium under the pines,
and who could bear azaleas, dogwood, early profuse rose
of somewhere else when you're assaulted here, early May,
not any calm narcissus, orange *corona*
on scalloped white, not even its slender stalk
in a fountain of leaves, no stiff cornets of the honest
jonquils, gendered parts upthrust in brass and cream:
just this common flash in anyone's yard,
scrambled cluster of petals
crayon-yellow, as in a child's drawing of the sun,
I'm bringing you a sun, a children's choir, host
of transient voices—wasn't it always
anyone's child you loved?—first bright
splash in the gray exhausted world, a feast
of the dooryard flower we call butter-and-egg.

ISLAND IN THE CHARLES

"By being scholar first of that new night"
— CRASHAW

Taking the well-worn path in the mind though dusk encroaches
upon the mind, taking back alleys careful step by step
past parked cars and trash containers, three blocks to the concrete ramp
of the footbridge spanning the highway with its rivering, four-lane
unstaunchable traffic, treading on shadow and slant broken light

my mother finds her way. By beer bottles, over smeared
Trojans, across leaf-muck, she follows the track, clutching her
jacket close. The footbridge lofts her over the flashing cars
and sets her down, gently, among trees, where she is a child
in the weave of boughs, and leafshapes plait the breeze.

She fingers silver-green blades of the crack willow, she tests dark grooves
of crack willow bark. The tree has a secret. Its branches pour
themselves back toward earth, and my mother pauses, dredging a breath
up out of her sluggish lungs. The blade leaves scratch
her fingertips, the corrugated bark

releases a privacy darker than cataract veils.
But slashed and ribboned, glimpsed through fronds,
the river hauls its cargo of argent light
and she advances, past basswood and crabapple clumps
along the tarmac where cyclists, joggers, rollerbladers

entranced in their varying orbits swoop
around her progress. With method, she reaches her bench,
she stations there. She sits columnular, fastened
to her difficult breath, and faces the river in late afternoon.
Behind her, voices. Before her, the current casts its glimmering

seine to a shore so distant no boundary scars
her retina, and only occasional sculls or sailboats flick

across her vision as quickened, condensing light.
There she sits, poised, while the fluent transitive Charles
draws off to the harbor and, farther, to the unseen sea

until evening settles, and takes her in its arms.

DAY LILIES

For six days, full-throated, they praised
the light with speckled tongues and blare
    of silence by the porch stair:
honor guard with blazons and trumpets raised
still heralding the steps of those
    who have not for years walked here
    but who once, pausing, chose

this slope for a throng of lilies:
and hacked with mattock, pitching stones
    and clods aside to tamp dense
clumps of bog-soil for new roots to seize.
So lilies tongued the brassy air
    and cast it back in the sun's
    wide hearing. So, the pair

who planted the bulbs stood and heard
that clarion silence. We've heard it,
    standing here toward sunset
as those gaping, burnished corollas poured
their flourish. But the petals have
    shriveled, from each crumpled knot
    droops a tangle of rough

notes shrunk to a caul of music.
Extend your palms: you could as well
    cup sunbeams as pour brim-full
again those absent flowers, or touch the quick
arms of those who bent here, trowel in
    hand, and scraped and sifted soil
    held in a bed of stone.

MARCH SNOW

Will it be gentle as this slow down-drifting
of the last flakes of winter, our separation?
The last one, I mean. The one we imagine
in a hospital room, with dim machines humming.
I hardly think so. Here outside my window
March wafts into extinction
as snow clumps melt from the roof and lapse
from boughs like loosened shawls falling.
All this in silence. The damp street steams.
This morning the house clamored with children
yanking brushes through hair, pulling on extra socks,
then suddenly the door slammed and out they went
into the soft, illusory drifts of early spring,
their lunchboxes swinging primary yellow and blue
against the belated white, small boots stamping a trail
that will melt into the future by late afternoon.

LOW BLUE FIRE

Late March, Vermont. Birds want fat and seeds.
Enormous cakes of suet don't last two weeks.
Look close: you'll almost see them burning it.
Face to face with scarcity, life's barely lit,
the birds' dull furnaces don't glow.
Banked too much to cast much shadow,
life crouches by the fire and shivers.
Today a dull brown thing with feathers
smacked my window, dazed and cold.
Warmth and darkness would, I hope,
revive its will to live. I got my coat
and looked outside, but, bird or ghost
was gone. Soon winter will fly too, and spring
will come in flocks of hungry, driven things.

VISITING MY PARENTS: NATICK, MASSACHUSETTS

When I *go home,*
Father fills me in on what's happened in our town,
and on my high-school boyfriend who trims the trees for him,

as if he thinks I still wonder
about David, a boy I never even kissed, the pure way I once saw
the world made me stiffen when he said he loved me, and answer

as if you know what that means.
Now, I stay up late when I go back, never doing any of the work
I bring along. Instead I climb the old trees, and through the branches

I see that young girl everywhere:
on the street late at night, hand in hand with David.
My big remembering brain shines down on her

    like a fat full moon,
illuminating everything, and I hang in the past, radiant, suspended, and
speechless, still undecided what to tell her, or what it means.

SNOW IN NEW HAMPSHIRE

All afternoon the children welcomed the snow
with their whole bodies, crawling in it, letting it touch
all the skin they can bear to have touched,
tossing, smoothing, shaping a new race of creatures
to guard the yard where they are at home,
white and lopsided, kindly, big-bellied,
like the first body they can remember wanting to touch.
The backyard slowly altered so utterly
by the accumulation of small flakes:
every limb and leaf of each tree outlined in white, even
the last apples, red remnants of the growing season.
Light so diffused it seems to come from everywhere and does.
Serious, absorbed, the children forget where they are,
they could be anywhere, which speaks to the pure freedom of this
    moment.
Its memory will return to them late one afternoon
many years from now in a city they haven't been to yet
as they walk home along a snowy street
and hearing children, stop to listen,
forget for that moment where they're going.

ZEA

Once their fruit is picked,
The cornstalks lighten, and though
Keeping to their strict

Rows, begin to be
The tall grasses that they are—
Lissom, now, and free

As canes that clatter
In island wind, or plumed reeds
Rocked by lake-water.

Soon, if not cut down,
Their ranks grow whistling-dry, and
Blanch to lightest brown,

So that, one day, all
Their ribbon-like, down-arcing
Leaves rise up and fall

In tossed companies,
Like goose-wings beating southward
Over the changed trees.

Later, there are days
Full of bare expectancy,
Downcast hues, and haze,

Days of an utter
Calm, in which one white corn-leaf,
Oddly a-flutter,

Its fabric sheathing
A gaunt stem, can seem to be
The sole thing breathing.

MAYFLIES

In somber forest, when the sun was low,
I saw from unseen pools a mist of flies
   In their quadrillions rise
And animate a ragged patch of glow
With sudden glittering—as when a crowd
     Of stars appear
Through a brief gap in black and driven cloud,
One arc of their great round-dance showing clear.

It was no muddled swarm I witnessed, for
In *entrechats* each fluttering insect there
   Rose two steep yards in air,
Then slowly floated down to climb once more,
So that they all composed a manifold
     And figured scene,
And seemed the weavers of some cloth of gold,
Or the fine pistons of some bright machine.

Watching those lifelong dancers of a day
As night closed in, I felt myself alone
   In a life too much my own,
More mortal in my separateness than they—
Unless, I thought, I had been called to be
     Not fly or star
But one whose task is joyfully to see
How fair the fiats of the caller are.

SIGNATURES

False Solomon's Seal—
So called because it lacks a
Star-scar on the heel,

And ends its arched stem
In a spray of white florets,
Later changing them

To a red, not blue,
Spatter of berries—is no
Falser than the true.

Solomon, who raised
The temple and wrote the song,
Wouldn't have dispraised

This bowed, graceful plant
So like an aspergillum,
Nor its variant

With root duly scarred,
Whose bloom-hung stem is like the
Bell-branch of a bard.

Liking best to live
In the deep woods whose light is
Most contemplative,

Both are often found
Where mandrake, wintergreen, and
Dry leaves strew the ground,

Their heads inclining
Toward the dark earth, one blessing
And one divining.

CROW'S NESTS

That lofty stand of trees beyond the field,
Which in the storms of summer stood revealed

As a great fleet of galleons bound our way
Across a moiled expanse of tossing hay,

Full-rigged and swift, and to the topmost sail
Taking their fill and pleasure of the gale,

Now, in this leafless time, are ships no more,
Though it would not be hard to take them for

A roadstead full of naked mast and spar
In which we see now where the crow's nests are.

THE EXODUS OF PEACHES

The new peach trees are bandaged
like the legs of stallions.

You can read the bark
over the tape's white lip

where its russet Braille
is peeling. The peaches hang

in their green cupolas,
cheeks stained with twilight,

the wind stenciled on velvet
livery. What a traffic

of coaches without wheels,
of bells without tongues!

Far off the barn doors
open, close,

open, close.
An argument,

both sides swinging.
The blue tractor zippers the field

and disappears behind slatted boxes
like weathered shingles, stained

with peach juice.
I stood under peaches

clumped close as barnacles,
loyal as bees,

and picked one
from the only life it knew.

THE PUMP

Drawing water, three short down-strokes
  on the pitcher pump inside the house,
  five staunch clanging down-strokes
  on the long-neck pump outside,
  gush.

Carrying water in a bucket carefully
  so as not to spill.

Striking a match to light the kindling scraps,
  the first flame blue and soft.

Filling the lamps with kerosene,
  feeling darkness coming so gently.

Washing hands in a metal basin.

Bringing in firewood, the weight of the logs
  seeming to drive the body forward.

Sitting on the back porch,
  watching wind ruffle the aspen leaves.

Day and night were dust settling on a shelf,
  dreamlessly content.

Sometimes when I stepped outside I thought
  I might greet some wayfarers:
  people who were still on foot.

I would shake their hands, hear them speak
  their unamplified words, offer them bread
  baked in the cook stove, stroll a ways
  together down the unlit road.

Nothing but time breathing,
   stars,
     stony earth beneath our feet.

Nothing but the pump and water—
   cold and deeper than any voice.

CHEERFUL

Not passable, not special, not ostensible,
But cheerful, as in rising in the winter darkness
Of a northern morning and, while walking down
The worn, bare-wood stairs to the kitchen and
   The cold cookstove, whistling

For the sake of being in a relatively warm body,
For the sake of sliding fingers along the smooth rail,
For the sake of being eager to start a fire exactly
As she liked to start it with shredded
   Newspaper, split kindling

And a bit of birch bark and there it went—
The glow, a tiny whiff of smoke, and the ardent
Promise of heat. Cheerful in her mind that knew
Which pan to take down, how much butter to put
   In that pan, how many days'

Butter was left in the fridge, how much butter
Cost at the A & P, cheerful for looking out the window
At ice-whiskered nothingness and knowing there would be
A day, an event sponsored by galaxies, God,
   And gravity—choose one or choose

Them all—all were plausible. Sunlight was a hymn, though
She knew more than to tell the preacher. Half-overalled
Husband cranky, the boys cuffing each other and muttering
Mocking words beneath their sleep-furred breath
   And she cheerful to their faces

Like an opera singer exiled by catastrophe
To some cowtown who rose in the shivery, blank morning
And sat on the edge of her gray, narrow bed
And began—despite herself and because of herself—
    To whistle an intractable aria.

TIME OF YEAR

It is a morning
                    But you must tell the time of year

It is a morning in late March
There is much yearning for spring
The chickadees are singing, the buds on the lilacs feel hard
But not quite as hard as in January
                                    That is
Probably not true but wanting affects our perceptions

It should affect them
Particularly on a gray chill morning
When snow stands in random
                                No not random
But according to the exactions of sun and shade

Stands then in clots in the open area
Around the house and the brown grass is weak,
Discouraged, plaintive, wan
When a moose
                    Patchy clots of fur, that devout,
Deep look of animal indifference,
A cow, not stilts for legs but long legs nevertheless
So that walking seems to be assaying the ground
Step by step

Ambles into the yard
The largest animate presence we have laid eyes on
Since we visited the zoo in Baltimore two summers ago

Gray to deep brown hide mottled with black
Not a uniform color

We stare out the window at the beleaguered beauty
Of ungainliness

She's an old hairy woman, you say
What I am going to be, you say

The moose moves on toward the fir thickets out back

The snow fleas are lovely too, you say
Later as we tramp down the road in search of pussy willows

They form almost solid black masses
Upon puddles of melted snow

It is all too much, you say and stop in the road
And fling your arms in a gesture of welcome,
Thanksgiving, passion, bereavement, feeling

BUILDING A HOUSE IN THE WOODS, MAINE, 1971

A good uphill mile and a half from a not very good
                                    dirt road,
That distance on foot meaning a sort of mincing strut
                                    over frost heaves
And washouts across what had been a poor road at best
                                    fifty years previously,
Through tangles of witch hazel, alder and birch saplings
                                    and—at this time
Of year in the low spots—sucking gurgling mud:
                                    that expedition
Taking the better part of an hour to a ridge side where
                                    a few gaunt disheartened
Apple trees and dead elms from the nineteenth century
                                    stood like blank-eyed

Sentinels and where you intended to build a house
                                    that would stare
Without curtains at a prospect of more ridges and then
                                    real mountains that
Receded to a tangible approximation of geographic eternity.

And why shouldn't love be made here, meals cooked and
                                    consumed, fires stoked,
Children born who would have the endless woods to frolic in,
                                    who would be free
In a way our world no longer allowed anyone to feel?
                                    Weren't we all
Young and able to split, hammer, haul, plant, saw, push,
                                    carry, lift, and
At the end of the physical day simply and sublimely sit?

We breathed the dank clean air, the thin sharp smells of
                                    pine woods and dead
Leaves and melting snow and we started to whoop and jig
                                    for the vision of it,
The abiding strength that we had gone too long without.

Contributors

JULIA ALVAREZ is Writer-in-Residence at Middlebury College, the author of numerous novels and collections of poetry, including *How the Garcia Girls Lost Their Accents* and *In the Time of the Butterflies*.

PETER BALAKIAN edits Graham House Review and teaches at Colgate University. His numerous volumes include, most recently, *June-tree: New and Selected Poems, 1974–2000*.

JENNIFER BATES graduated from Princeton University and has published a volume of poems entitled *The First Night Out of Eden*. She currently lives in Middlebury, Vermont.

PHILIP BOOTH lives in Maine. His many books include *Lifelines: Selected Poems, 1950–1999, Pairs,* and *Selves*.

T. ALAN BROUGHTON teaches at the University of Vermont. His books of poetry include *In the Country of Elegies, Preparing to Be Happy,* and *Dreams Before Sleep*.

ROSELLEN BROWN, a well-known novelist and poet, is the author of *Cora Fry's Pillow Book,* a long poem, and *A Rosellen Brown Reader*.

DAVID BUDBILL is a poet and playwright who lives in Vermont. His past titles include *Judevine* and *Moment to Moment*.

JOHN CANADAY won the Walt Whitman Award from the Academy of American Poets for his first book of poems, *The Invisible World*. His most recent work is a critical study entitled *The Nuclear Muse: Literature, Physics, and the First Atomic Bombs*.

LESLEY DAUER teaches in the English Department at Foothill College. Her latest book is *The Fragile City*.

PETER DAVISON is poetry editor of *The Atlantic* and the author of many volumes of poetry. His most recent volume is entitled *Breathing Room*.

GREG DELANTY is an Irishman who teaches at St. Michael's College in Vermont and has published numerous collections of poetry, including *The Hellbox*.

MARK DOTY, a well-known poet and memoirist, divides his time between Provincetown, Massachusetts, and Salt Lake City, Utah.

JOHN ENGELS teaches at St. Michael's College in Vermont and is the author of numerous volumes of poetry, including *Sinking Creek* and *Walking to Cootehill*.

CAROL FROST lives in Otego, New York and teaches at Hartwick College in Oneonta.

RICHARD FROST is a professor of English at the State University College at Oneonta, New York.

JEFFREY HARRISON was recently a poet-in-residence at Phillips Andover Academy. He is the author of *The Singing Underneath, Signs of Arrival,* and *Secondhand Ecstasy.*

LABAN CARRICK HILL has published many novels for children. He lives in Burlington, Vermont.

DAVID HUDDLE teaches at the University of Vermont. He has published many collections of short fiction and poetry, and has recently published a novel entitled *The Story of a Million Years.*

CYNTHIA HUNTINGTON teaches at Dartmouth College. Her books include *The Salt House* and *We Have Gone to the Beach.*

RICHARD JACKSON teaches at the University of Tennessee at Chattanooga. His most recent publications include *Hartwall* and *Half Lives: Petrarchan Poems.*

ERICA JONG is a novelist and poet, author of *Becoming Light,* a recent volume of selected poems. Her many novels include *Fear of Flying* and *Fanny.*

RICHARD KENNEY, a former McArthur Fellow, is the author of *The Invention of the Zero, Orrery,* and other volumes. He has a home in western Vermont but currently teaches at the University of Washington.

GALWAY KINNELL, a Pulitzer Prize winning poet, was Poet Laureate of Vermont.

MAXINE KUMIN is a distinguished poet, novelist, and essayist who lives in rural New Hampshire. Her books include *Always Beginning* and *Connecting the Dots.*

SYDNEY LEA was founding editor of *New England Review.* A poet, novelist, and essayist, his many volumes of poetry include *To the Bone* and *Pursuit of a Wound.*

BRAD LEITHAUSER teaches at Mount Holyoke College and has published novels and volumes of poetry, including *Hundreds of Fireflies.*

GARY MARGOLIS is a clinical psychologist at Middlebury College and the author of several collections of poetry.

PAUL MARIANI has published numerous volumes of poetry as well as biographies of Hart Crane, William Carlos Williams, John Berrymann, and Robert Lowell.

CLEOPATRA MATHIS teaches at Dartmouth College. Among her recent books are *Guardian* and *What to Tip the Boatman.*

GARDNER MCFALL lives in New York City. Her first collection of poetry is entitled *The Pilot's Daughter.* She recently edited *Made with Words,* a collection of the prose of Mary Swenson.

WESLEY MCNAIR teaches at the University of Maine at Farmington. Her books include *Twelve Journeys in Maine* and the forthcoming *Mapping the Heart.*

NORA MITCHELL lives in Burlington, Vermont, and has published several collections of poetry, including *Your Skin Is a Country* and *Proofreading the Histories.*

SUSAN MITCHELL is an award winning poet and a professor at Florida Atlantic University. Her books include *Rapture* and *Eroticon.*

NANCY NAHRA teaches at Champlain College in Burlington, Vermont. Her most recent collection of poetry is entitled *More Charming.*

ALFRED NICOL lives in Amesbury, Massachusetts, where he has worked for many years as a printer. A graduate of Dartmouth College, he has just finished his first volume of poems, *Penumbra*.

CAROLE SIMMONS OLES teaches at California State University, Chico. Her publications include *The Loneliness Factor* and *Sympathetic Systems*.

APRIL OSSMANN is director of Alice James Books and teaches creative writing and literature at the University of Maine at Farmington. She has published poetry in numerous journals including *Harvard Review, Seneca Review,* and *Prairie Schooner*.

ROBERT PACK taught for nearly four decades at Middlebury College and was director of the Bread Loaf Writers' Conference for many years. He has published over a dozen volumes of poetry.

JAY PARINI, a poet, novelist, and biographer, teaches at Middlebury College. His most recent volumes of poetry are *Town Life* and *House of Days*.

JOEL B. PECKHAM, JR. is a graduate of Middlebury College who has just begun to publish his poems in national magazines.

KEVIN PILKINGTON teaches at Sarah Lawrence College and the New School for Social Research. His latest volume of poems is *Spare Change*.

VERANDAH PORCHE lives in Vermont. She has published numerous volumes of poetry.

LAWRENCE RAAB teaches at Williams College. His books include *The Collector of Cold Weather* and *The Probable World*.

IRA SADOFF teaches at Colby College in Maine and has published many books of poetry, including *Emotional Traffic* and *Grazing*.

MARY JO SALTER teaches at Mount Holyoke College and is the author of numerous volumes of poetry, including *A Kiss in Space*.

NEIL SHEPARD lives in Vermont and edits *Green Mountain Review*.

JANE SHORE lives in Vermont and Maryland. Her many volumes of poetry include *Music Minus One* and *Happy Family*.

ROBERT SIEGEL once taught at Dartmouth College and now teaches at the University of Wisconsin in Milwaukee. He has published numerous volumes of poetry, including *In a Pig's Eye*.

DIANE SWAN's latest publication is entitled *Jewelweed*.

JOHN TAGLIABUE currently lives in Rhode Island. He recently published his *New and Selected Poems: 1942–1997*.

SUE ELLEN THOMPSON is a freelance writer and editor living in Mystic, Connecticut. Her most recent work, *The Leaving: New and Selected Poems,* was nominated for a Pulitzer Prize.

PAULS TOUTONGHI is a recent graduate of Middlebury College who is pursuing graduate study at Cornell University. His poems and stories have begun to appear in national magazines, including the *Boston Review*.

ELLEN BRYANT VOIGT is currently the Poet Laureate of Vermont.

ROSANNA WARREN teaches at Boston University and is the author of several volumes of poetry. She recently spent a year in Rome at the American Academy.

EMILY WHEELER is a Dartmouth College graduate who has published poems in many journals. She currently lives in Germany.

RICHARD WILBUR is a former Poet Laureate of the United States.

NANCY WILLARD teaches at Vassar College and has published numerous novels, books for children, and volumes of poetry.

BARON WORMSER is currently the Poet Laureate of Maine. His books include *Mulroney and Others* and *When*.

(continued from page iv)

Greg Delanty, "A Wake on Lake Champlain" and "Vermont Aisling," originally published in *American Wake* (Dufour, Ireland: Blackstaff Press); "The Great Ship" appeared in *Metre,* Dublin, Ireland.

Mark Doty, "American Sublime" appeared in *Poetry Review* (U.K.); "Time on Main" in *Source*.

John Engels, "Bleeding Heart," appeared in *Maine Times;* "Raking the Leaves," originally published in *Sinking Creek* (New York: The Lyons Press), 1998; "Moving from Williston," appeared in *Kenyon Review;* "Storm," originally published in *Big Water* (New York: Lyons and Burford), 1994.

Carol Frost, "Country," "Flicker," and "Winter Poem," originally published in *Love and Scorn, New and Selected Poems,* Triquarterly Books/Northwestern University Press.

Richard Frost, "The Change," appeared in *The Paris Review;* "The Hill," in *Controlled Burn*.

Jeffrey Harrison, "Horseshoe Contest" and "Not Written on Birch Bark," originally published in *Feeding the Fire,* Sarabaud Books, 2001.

David Huddle, "Idaho Once," appeared in *Maine Times;* "The Nature of Learning" originally published in *Summer Lake: New and Selected Poems,* LSU Press, 1999.

Richard Jackson, "The Angels of 1912 and 1972," is used by permission of the author and Cleveland State University Press; "Villanelle of the Crows" and "No Fault Love" are used by permission of the author and University of Massachusetts Press.

Richard Kenney, "Starling," "Driving Sleeping People," "Plume," and "Apples on Champlain," originally published in *Orrery,* Atheneum, 1985.

Galway Kinnell, "Trees" from *Imperfect Thirst* by Galway Kinnell. Copyright © 1994 by Galway Kinnell. Reprinted by permission of Houghton Mifflin Company. All rights reserved.

Maxine Kumin, "The Exchange," appeared in *The Massachusetts Review;* "The Potato Sermon," in *River City Review;* "Skinnydipping With William Wadsworth," in *The Hudson Review;* all were originally published in *The Long Marriage,* W. W. Norton, 2001.

Sydney Lea, "Inviting the Moose: A Vision," "Yoked Together," and "Well, Everything," originally published in *From Pursuit of a Wound,* University of Illinois Press, Urbana, 2000.

Gary F. Margolis, "Slow Words for Shoreham and the Apple Blossom Derby" and "First Spring," originally published in *Falling Awake,* University of Georgia Press, Athens Georgia, 1986.

Paul Mariani, "North/South," originally published in *Salvage Operations: New and Selected Poems,* W. W. Norton & Company, 1996; "Mountain View With Figures," "Landscape With Dog," and "New England Winter," originally published in *The Great Wheel,* W. W. Norton & Company, 1996; "A Break in the Weather," originally published in *Prime Mover,* Grove Press, 1985.

Cleopatra Mathis, "Gatekeeper," "The Owl," and "Intermediary" appeared in *River Styx* and were published in *What To Tip the Boatman?,* Sheep Meadow Press, 2001.

Gardner McFall, "Seaweed Weather," appeared in *The New Criterion*.

Wesley McNair, "Driving North in Winter," appeared in *The Kenyan Review;* "What They Are," in *The Virginia Quarterly Review;* "Shovels," in *The Swanee Review*.

Nora Mitchell, "Listening Through Snow," appeared in *Green Mountain Review*.

Susan Mitchell, "The Grove at Nemi" and "Pussy Willow," originally published in *Eroticon,* Harper Collins, 2000; "The Kiss," originally published in *Rapture,* Harper Collins, 1992.

Alfred Nicol, "Wide Brush," appeared in *Rattapallax*.

Carole Simmons Oles, "Old Couple at Howard Johnson's Soda Fountain in Manchester, New Hampshire" and "At Boston Public Library," originally published in *The Loneliness Factor,* Texas Tech University Press; "On the Cliff Walk at Newport, Rhode Island Thinking of Percy Bysshe Shelley," appeared in *Indiana Review;* "Apple-Picking," appeared in *Prairie Schooner;* "After Fire in Ripton, Vermont," originally published in *Stunts,* Green-Tower Press.

April Ossmann, "Living Without," appeared in *Cincinnati Poetry Review;* "January Thaw," appeared in *the eleventh MUSE.*

Joel Peckham, "When I Dream of Eternity," "Mud Season," and "Cage Cry—Sharon Massachusetts," originally published in *Nightwalking,* Pecan Grove Press, 2001.

Kevin Pilkington, "Woodstock, Vermont" and "A Spruce in Vermont," originally published in *Spare Change,* La Jolla Poets Press, 1997.

Verandah Porche, "Villanelle in April," originally published in *Reading Matters,* Vermont Center for the Book.

Lawrence Raab, "Emily Dickinson's House" and "Hunters," originally published in *The Probable World,* Penguin, 2000.

Ira Sadoff, "The Horse Wanted Sugar," "I Join the Sparrows," and "I Like Waking Up," originally published in *Grazing: Poems,* copyright 1998 by Ira Sadoff. Used with permission of the University of Illinois Press.

Mary Jo Salter, "Spring Thaw in South Hadley," "Reading Room," and "The Upper Story," originally published in *Unfinished Painting,* by Mary Jo Salter, Knopf, 1989.

Jane Shore, "Public Service is Rich Enough" and "Fairbanks Museum and Planetarium," originally published in *Happy Family,* Picador USA, 1999.

Diane Swan, "Afterbirth," originally published in *Jewelweed,* State Street Press; "Wild Cedars," appeared in *Yankee.*

Sue Ellen Thompson, "Connecticut in March" and "Compass," copyright © 2001 by Sue Ellen Thompson. Reprinted by permission of Autumn House Press and the author.

Ellen Bryant Voigt, "A Brief Domestic History," appeared in *Triquarterly;* "The Art of Distance, I," in *Five Points,* will be collected in *Shadow of Heaven,* scheduled for February '02 publication with W. W. Norton; "Ravenous," in *Five Points;* "Dooryard Flower" in *The Atlantic Monthly.*

Richard Wilbur, "Crows Nest," "Zea," and "Mayflies," originally appeared in *The New Yorker;* "Signatures" in *The New Republic.* All four poems were published in *Mayflies,* Harcourt, 2000.

Nancy Willard, "The Exodus of Peaches," © 1996 by Nancy Willard, originally published in *Swimming Lessons: New and Selected Poems,* by Nancy Willard, Knopf, 1996.

Baron Wormser, "Cheerful," appeared in *Barrow Street;* "Building a House in the Woods, Maine, 1971," in the *Maine Times.*